WALLY ADAMCHIK, MBA, CMC

CONSTRUCTION
LEADERSHIP FROM
A Z TO

26 WORDS TO LEAD BY

LIVE OAK
BOOK COMPANY

Published by Live Oak Book Company
Austin, TX
www.liveoakbookcompany.com

Distributed by Live Oak Book Company

For ordering information or special discounts for bulk purchases, please contact Live Oak Book Company at PO Box 91869, Austin, TX 78709, 512.891.6100.

Design and composition by Greenleaf Book Group LLC and Alex Head
Cover design by Greenleaf Book Group LLC

Publisher's Cataloging-In-Publication Data
(Prepared by The Donohue Group, Inc.)

Adamchik, Wally.
   Construction leadership from A to Z : 26 words to lead by / Wally Adamchik.
— 1st ed.
   p. ; cm.
   Issued also as an ebook.
   ISBN: 978-1-936909-16-2
   1. Construction industry—Management. 2. Leadership. I. Title.

HD9715.A2 A33 2011
624.068   2011932069

Print ISBN: 978-1-936909-16-2
eBook ISBN: 978-1-936909-17-9

First Edition

CONTENTS

INTRODUCTION

A few years ago I wrote a book on leadership. Now here I am writing another one. My doubting self wonders if books on leadership are like cookbooks. Do they get purchased, looked at once, and shelved for posterity? My positive self knows the study of leadership is an ongoing process. It is a journey of discovery: discovery of self, of others, and of emerging ideas on the subject. My business consultant self knows my earlier book was described as "one of the best business books of 2007" by *Entrepreneur* magazine. I know from my consulting and coaching work that people are thirsty for quality leadership, and they are looking for help. This book is a direct response to their searching.

I wish I could tell you that you hold in your hands a completely revolutionary approach to leadership, one that will change your life. Alan Webber, founding editor of *Fast Company* magazine, knows you'd like to shake things up at work. He said, "It is true that management in the United States has a tendency to look for silver bullets and fads." There are no silver bullets here. In fact, you have seen some of this ammo before. You have unpacked it, considered it, and either put it to use or, more likely, repacked it—and there is the problem. When we see something repeatedly, we tend not to pay attention to it. When we hear the same story over and over again, it fails to resonate with us the way it did the first time. The words and concepts you will read are ones you have read before. *Don't discount them.* Your challenge is to see them again for the very first time. The bigger challenge is to apply them in your life *now*.

Like many authors, I plodded along on this book for a while. Then I witnessed an exchange between a consultant and the CEO of my biggest and most important client. The consultant was discussing a presentation he had just delivered to the staff of this organization. It wasn't a bad presentation. In fact, it was rather like a dress rehearsal for a presentation to be given several months later to nearly one thousand managers of this company. I was in the room because I was the program manager for the event. The CEO made a minor comment about some wording the consultant had used. The consultant replied that he recognized that the wording might not be quite right, but when he wrote his book thirteen years ago, that was the wording he had chosen, and he hasn't changed it since. The conversation ended soon after, and the consultant left, happy with his performance.

The CEO fired him that afternoon. While there were several reasons for this, the CEO's comment that remains most prominent in my mind is this: "He wrote a book thirteen years ago. What? He hasn't done anything since then?" I resolved right then and there to get this book finished! But the deeper point is the one we must address: *Things change. People change.* We learn and we evolve. Legendary motivational speaker, the late Charles E. (Tremendous) Jones, often said, "Five years from now, you'll be the same person you are today—except for the books you read and the people you meet." Surely this consultant had read some books and met some people. The CEO expected him, as a professional, to *continue to develop.* He didn't. This brings us to you.

Are you like that consultant? Or do you recognize the truth spoken by Charlie Jones? Because you hold this book in your hands, I presume the latter. I know you are busy and face competing demands for your time every day. With that in mind, I have written this book in a manner that will allow you to complete a chapter in thirty minutes or less. You can pick it up at any point; each chapter stands alone. The twenty-six chapter titles represent characteristics we often associate with successful leaders.

I didn't select these words. I merely developed a list of possible titles for each letter and then surveyed people like you: managers out there in the trenches every day. The words you will read about are qualities that resonated with learners and leaders like yourself. I just expounded on the list they created.

One thing we know about leaders is that they make new leaders. This book is ideal for helping you in that endeavor. In fact, in the chapter called "Genuine" you will read about a book club that one company created to help develop its people. This book provides you with twenty-six sessions of leadership conversations. If you do one every other week, you have a year of learning. These sessions can be done over lunch and in small groups. They don't cost a lot of money, but the payoff can be substantial.

Whether you read chapters alone or within a group, the challenge is clear. Are you getting better at what you do? What are you learning? What changes are you making to be more successful in the coming years? As we enter the second decade of the twenty-first century, we need better leaders. The demands are great, but they are not insurmountable. In fact, people and firms are meeting these demands every day. These are companies that are led by strong, flexible leaders who choose to continue to learn and grow.

I am making the journey with you. Research for this project confirmed much of what I knew, but I also picked up some new ideas and did some self-improvement work along the way. I hope the same happens for you. Let me know.

Stay inspired.

ATTITUDE

There is little difference in people, but that little difference makes a big difference. The little difference is attitude. The big difference is whether it is positive or negative. —W. Clement Stone

at·ti·tude - Disposition; feeling; orientation, esp. of the mind

___

What would you do to someone who kept talking trash about you and to you? Everything you did was wrong and everything that happened to you was going to turn out bad? You say "yes;" they say "no." You say "black;" they say "white." You say "I can;" they say "you can't." I hope you would get that person out of your life. However, we all have that doubting voice inside of us to some extent. The winners in the world are able to silence the negative voice and listen only to the positive voice.

Leaders impact people. This is external, but everything you do is based on how you think and feel *internally*. Ultimately it is your attitude that determines much of your success: your attitudes about yourself, your employees, a given situation, the market, and so on. And, of course, you are responsible for, and *can choose*, your attitude.

There are a number of excellent books on success that focus on this concept. *Think and Grow Rich* by Napoleon Hill and *As a Man Thinketh* by James Allen are two that readily come to mind and warrant further study. Allen states, "a man is literally what he thinks, his character being the complete sum of all his thoughts." If someone is inclined to think poorly of people and situations, they will generally experience poor outcomes. Conversely, a positive attitude has the potential to create positive outcomes. In the physical world we accept, and expect, that a tomato will create tomato seeds that will, in turn, create more tomatoes. A gorilla will give birth to a gorilla, and so forth. What then of ideas and attitudes? They are no different. Good ideas and attitudes give birth to good results.

Leaders can't really have "bad days." This is not to say you should be walking around singing "Zippity-Doo-Dah" every day. That would be inappropriate and would deny the seriousness of the issues you face. You will have bad moments, but you must adjust your attitude and quickly get back on the right track. Your people can't have a bad day because you are having one. What happens with one employee in the morning should not color the conversation you have with another employee in the afternoon. An old saying contends that "if mama ain't happy, ain't nobody happy." We can safely modify that here to say that "if the boss isn't happy, nobody is happy." It's your choice, and it comes from your attitude.

There are a number of steps you can take to work on improving your attitude. To begin thinking more positively, simply look for and embrace the good. As noted earlier, read *Think and Grow Rich* and other inspiring texts, and associate with positive, productive people.

Then get rid of the negative. Nothing can ruin your good attitude faster than a group of cynical friends or associates who are quick to complain about anything. These "sucking holes of negativity" are like black holes in the universe—they suck in our energy and wear us down. Steer clear of them. They are often found in breakrooms and office kitchens doing more complaining than working. Avoid these people at all costs.

You must get rid of other negative influences as well. We are surrounded by noise, self-appointed "experts" telling us what we should be thinking and feeling. Cut the noise. Talk radio, the Internet, and a few hundred cable television channels can be on the top of your *Things Not to Do* list. It is impossible to think clearly and maintain a positive attitude when your brain is continually filtering out noise and unnecessary information. Find a way to give yourself some space so your brain can do the hard work of thinking for itself and helping you maintain your positive attitude. If this concept is of interest to you, I invite you to read *Why Is Everyone So Cranky* by Leslie Charles.

For many people, the first step toward improving job performance is improving how they feel about themselves. Researcher J. R. Gribble notes that, for 8 in 10 people, self-image matters more in how they rate job performance than their actual job performance. In other words, their attitude about themselves plays a big part in their job satisfaction and performance. Not only that, a positive outlook can help you stay healthy. A study of 124 first-year law students confirmed that when optimism increased, so did immune system function. The converse was true also. When optimism decreased, so did the immune system function. This research has been repeated elsewhere with similar results. We now understand that the immune system is not a stand-alone system. It is closely integrated with our nervous system, which is closely integrated with our brains and attitudes.

Further, it is more the sum total of thoughts and experiences that matters. An event may be crucial in the short term, but researchers find that people's *enduring self-concept*—their view of who they are and what they are capable of—is not tied to any single positive or negative event. As you can see, a positive attitude is not a part-time decision. We must work at it continually. The payoff is a higher likelihood of employees who look to the positive and, therefore, more positive things happening for you and your company.

A positive attitude may not solve all your problems, but it will annoy enough people to make it worth the effort. —Herm Albright

ATTITUDE IN ACTION

Fran Burke is the vice president of operations for Faulconer Construction. Faulconer specializes in site work and horizontal infrastructure projects in the Southeast. I have known Fran for a decade, and he has always struck me as one of the most positive people I have ever known. He was the logical person to talk to about attitude. As with all fine leaders, he took the opportunity to point out someone from his team rather than shine the light on himself. Here are some of his comments:

> We first brought Mindy to Faulconer as an intern. Talk about a challenge; she was our first intern, and she was female. As you know, there are some in this industry who haven't fully come into the twenty-first century as it relates to gender equality, but she shrugged off all of this and

simply went to work. We were so impressed, we invited her back the next year and hired her when she graduated. She quickly learned the ropes and was ready to run a project. We assigned her to the Meadow Creek Parkway project. This was not your basic new road. It went through a park, and there was some heavy opposition to the project. Once we finally did get notice to proceed, railroad, trail, and utility conflicts kept popping up. Virginia DOT was the owner for this $15 million project. They did a fine job, but the bureaucracy can be frustrating when working with any level of government. This was all made worse by a small but vocal opposition to the job.

Mindy was up against a very difficult situation—injunctions, easements, and public outcry coupled with vandalism on the job that destroyed over $100,000 worth of equipment. And this was her first project as a project manager! I visited her at the jobsite one day early on. I made a comment about hanging in there or lasting until the end as part of my greeting. I will never forget her response. She said, very matter-of-factly, "I'm glad you assigned me to this project. I am truly thankful." "Oh really? Why is that?" I asked. "Because," the young project manager explained, "if I can manage this project, I can manage anything." What a great attitude. And she is getting it done. As the project nears successful completion, there is talk of it receiving special recognition from VDOT.

Certainly Mindy is skilled at her job, but what truly sets her apart, I was reminded that day, is her attitude.

A TO Z APPLICATION

1. On a scale of 1–10, how do you rate yourself on having a positive attitude? _____

2. Write how you would like to be described by people._____
   _____
   _____

3. List someone you know who exemplifies this trait: _____
   _____

4. Is your self-talk generally positive, neutral, or negative? _____
   _____
   _____

5. What action *will* you do to improve in this area?_____
   _____

ATTITUDE JUMPSTART

- Stay hydrated. Dehydration can make you confused, angry, tense, and blue.
- Make a list of things you are grateful for.
- Know that nothing will bother you. If it does, give it ten seconds, then move on.
- Smile.
- Read *Don't Sweat the Small Stuff . . . and It's All Small Stuff.*

BALANCE

To acquire balance means to achieve that happy medium between the minimum and the maximum that represents your optimum. The minimum is the least you can get by with. The maximum is the most you're capable of. The optimum is the amount or degree of anything that is most favorable toward the ends you desire. —Nido Qubein

bal·ance - A state of equilibrium; equal distribution of weight, amount, etc. / OPPOSITE - Imbalance; instability

———

For the leader, balance applies in three ways:

1. Self

2. Focus

3. Others

The *self* part is the balance we normally think of: the harmonious coexistence of family, work, recreation, and other important facets of our lives. When we give a disproportionate amount of attention to one area, our overall balance is at risk.

If you are an entrepreneur, the distinction between work and home is often murky. The rise of the PDA and now smartphone has aided in the decline of personal time for most managers. Intense competition and a 24/7 approach to business means work often eclipses everything else, including family.

In the short run, balance is nearly impossible. But in the long run, it is essential. When I was getting my MBA while working a full-time job, I wasn't able to spend much time with my family or to exercise for my health. That two-year period was out of balance for me on a personal level. But since then I have been able to devote much more time to both my family and to my workout regimen. Things are back in balance, and, for the long term, I am okay. When I have a major project due to a client that will take up more of my time, my balance may be temporarily skewed. That is why I calculate balance on a *quarterly* scale; day-to-day imbalances are corrected over a longer period.

Middle managers whose careers are flourishing are 53 percent more likely to engage in healthy lifestyle habits than those whose careers have stalled. Sales consultant and speaker Bill Brooks writes,

"Time on means time off. It is difficult to perform at peak levels if you are tired or dulled by overwork."

With our life balanced as best as we can presently make it, we turn to balance of *focus*. People in impact positions often function as leaders *and* managers. Each of us has our preferences and strengths and a comfort zone we like to operate in. The most successful leaders know the difference between leading and managing and are able to shift roles quickly and easily. Lee Scott, former CEO of Walmart, points out, "There's so much said today about leadership. But I don't think in business you can forget the fact that you don't just have to lead, you have to manage." Balance of focus says *we know what to do and when to do it.*

Balance with others is about operating fairly. The people you lead do not expect equal treatment. They generally understand and accept the nuances and accommodations made for people *if* this approach is applied to everyone you lead. If one person is always permitted to leave early because of personal issues, resentment will build. If all are permitted, when necessary, to adjust work hours to meet a personal need, this will be perceived as fair. Does one person always get the great assignments while another always gets the dogs? If these employees are equal in ability and performance, this will be viewed as unfair.

Balance applies to praise and critique also. Notice, we are not talking about giving equal measures of both but about giving each as necessary. Some bosses think praising a worker is coddling. Others think critiquing is confrontational. Both of these perspectives are wrong. The right approach is the balanced one.

It is equally important to foster balance in your employees. While it is not your primary responsibility to ensure balance in their lives, it is safe to say that if you don't pay attention to it your primary job will be negatively impacted. In 1971 about 15 percent of Marines were married. Today that number is 45 percent. General James T. Conway states, "We believe you recruit a Marine, but retain a family." Dan Braun, vice president of human resources at COLAS North America, is quick to recognize this. At the end of any multi-day training program he oversees, he delivers closing comments. He always tells the students to thank their families. He knows what General Conway knows: The families contribute to the success of what you are doing.

So how do you know if you are in balance? Deep down, you probably already know. But ask someone you trust for an honest opinion. Also, do you have goals set in all areas of your life? Are you making progress toward them on a regular basis? There are things I want to achieve in the physical, spiritual, family, career, financial, social, and mental aspects of my life, so I set annual goals. I check my progress quarterly (some would advocate monthly) and adjust as necessary to maintain progress in all areas. A vivid vision in your mind of a balanced future is the best way to create balance now.

Life is best enjoyed when time periods are evenly divided between labor, sleep, and recreation . . . all people should spend one-third of their time in recreation which is rebuilding, voluntary activity, never idleness. —Brigham Young

BALANCE IN ACTION

It was the middle of the construction boom of the early twenty-first century, and Hill and Wilkinson, a $270 million general contractor in the Dallas area, was seeing decreasing scores on employee satisfaction surveys. This was particularly true of employees with less than five years of experience. Employees were pointing out that long work hours were a problem. There is no doubt construction is known for long hours, but these employees were saying enough is enough.

With clear recognition that work hours were a problem, the company turned to its employees for ideas on how to correct the situation. One of the first things they did was to conduct training for senior managers about the importance of balance and the impact their behavior had on their employees. When senior managers put in long hours, it prompted junior employees to put in long hours. Seeing this, senior managers then would visit with employees, especially on late nights, and tell them to go home. But the senior manager often stayed and continued working. Junior employees heard one message, *go home*, but saw another, *stay and work*. Senior managers finally had to practice what they preached and leave at a decent hour also. This simple change gave permission to others to manage their time better.

At the project level, adjustments were made also, but the solution was left to the teams. One team found a way to work four ten-hour shifts, while another found a way to have team members rotate through, having Friday off.

The net result was an increase in employee satisfaction as employees found better balance in their lives. In fact, the *Dallas Business Journal* selected Hill and Wilkinson as one of the best places to work in the Dallas–Fort Worth area in 2007, 2008, 2009, and 2010. Companies creating a great place to work enjoy better financial performance than those who don't. Hill and Wilkinson remains an industry leader because of its commitment to employees.

A TO Z APPLICATION

1. Write your own definition of balance: _____

_____

_____

2. List someone you know who exemplifies this trait: _____

_____

_____

3. On a scale of 1–10, how do you rate on this trait? _____

_____

_____

4. Consider these major areas that might be important to you. In each of these how satisfied are you?

Family _____

Career _____

Financial _____

Fitness _____

Faith _____

Other_____

5. What action *will* you do to improve in this area?_____

_____

_____

BALANCE JUMPSTART

- Say no appropriately.
- Keep a food log for one week; adjust your eating habits to improve your balance.
- Get the right amount of sleep.
- Work on your marriage (or important relationships).
- Maintain and refer to your time log and analyze what you should be doing versus what you are doing.
- Read *The Long Life Equation.*

COMMUNICATE

The single biggest problem in communication is the illusion that it has taken place. —George Bernard Shaw

com·mu·ni·cate - To impart knowledge of; make known; to give or interchange thoughts, feelings, information, or the like, by writing, speaking, etc. / OPPOSITE - Conceal; withhold

———

Leaders get people to do things. These actions may be of the leader's choosing or they may be a shared objective, but the leader is the one who gets it all started. The leader is the one who helps people understand their role and their contribution. The leader tells the story and explains the "why." Author and Professor Nitin Nohria says communication is the real work of leadership, while presidential speechwriter James Humes contends the art of communication is the language of leadership. Most people think themselves much better communicators than they really are. My wife often reminds me of this failing.

In the past week or so, have there been instances where you found yourself thinking (or saying), "That was a misunderstanding"? It doesn't matter whose fault it was. What matters is that communication broke down. It was not effective. Notice we have not used the words *speaking* and *telling*. Communication is not about your monologue; it is about the message interpreted by the receiver matching the message intended by the sender. Effective communication means that what is heard is actually what was meant to be heard.

Communication is most effective when it flows evenly between people. Thus, listening is equally as important as speaking. The only way a leader can know what is going on in the ranks is to talk with people and be *genuinely interested* in what they tell him or her. This dialogue goes a long way to establish credibility for the leader. Listening sends the message, "I am interested in you and what you have to say." It says, "You matter to me and to this organization."

Many definitions of leadership include the word *influence*. Generally there are two ways in which a leader can influence others to do something. The first is by setting an example or modeling the desired behavior. The second is by communicating personally and organizationally to others to help them understand the vision, the objectives, and the plan. This helps people understand their role in accomplishing the objectives—why they are important and the impact they can have. Perhaps more important, effective communication also contains an element of motivation. Having clearly explained a group or individual's role in helping to achieve a goal, the right kind of communication can galvanize them into action.

The problem is that communicating is a skill we take for granted. Actually, we tend to ignore it. Consider where we first learn to communicate—at home. This environment may not have been the most conducive to learning clear, effective means of transmitting ideas. Then we went off to school where we may have picked up many bad communication habits. (For those of you who have sent children to preschool or kindergarten, you know what I mean. The vocabulary they come home with is sometimes not what you want them to have!)

When we finish school, we enter the workforce—replete with more opportunities for negative examples of communication. So by default rather than by intention we develop styles of communication that may include sarcasm, vagueness, indirectness, or other means of masking our true intent.

We each have a style of communicating. The DiSC Model of Dr. Ralph Marston is one of the easiest to apply and understand. It states that there are four basic types of communication styles. The four types entail a combination of people orientation and detail orientation. They have been called dominant, influential, steady, and critic. Radio frequencies are a useful analogy. If I am an FM transmitter and you are an AM receiver, all we have between us is static. If I am an FM transmitter on 105 and you are an FM receiver on 95, we still have static, but we now have a chance of communicating. If I adjust my setting to 95, I can now communicate with you on your wavelength. It is all about being adaptable in our own style of communication. These frequency adjustments are one of the keys to effective communication.

The most fundamental part of being human—the ability to communicate—is rarely taught to us. Many of you have taken speaking or presentation skills classes. Have you taken a listening skills class? Effective two-way communication is essential to the ultimate success of a leader. There are many things you can do to become a better communicator:

- First, understand your style. The DiSC assessment is an excellent tool for this.
- Second, study the subject. There are many books on how to improve your communication skills. Pick up one or two.
- Third, apply, analyze, and refine what you learn to become more effective.

Before we close this section, I must touch on technology. Several years ago, Richard Moran wrote a simple business book full of wisdom, *Never Confuse a Memo with Reality*. To his insights I would add, "Never confuse an e-mail (or text message) with effective communication." It *may* get the point across—but it may not. And in today's business climate, that's not a chance you can afford to take. Certainly, as Generation Y comes into the workforce, technology will continue to evolve. But what we know for sure is that communication happens best when it's face-to-face. An over-reliance on technology spells doom for most any leader.

Clear, open, effective communication is the bedrock of successful leadership. And, at its core, leadership is about relationships. Effective leaders have more effective and positive relationships. And like all relationships, good, ongoing communication is essential.

We have two ears and one mouth so that we can listen twice as much as we speak. —*Epictetus*

COMMUNICATION IN ACTION

The construction industry is a task-oriented mix of a drive for results with attention to detail. The people side of the equation is often missed and sometimes abused. Recognizing the importance of effective communication, Kinsley Construction lists Essentials of

Communication as a prerequisite for all subsequent courses at Kinsley University. All employees in supervisory roles attend a half-day session on communication. The highlight of this session is the DiSC profile. No single program will eliminate conflict, but this effort has increased the quality of communication by increasing awareness and giving attendees information they can use on the job to communicate more effectively.

Long time Kinsley employee, John Kotchish, has become one of the biggest supporters of the program. Here is what he says:

This is a great tool for zeroing in on how different folks operate, think, and how they respond in a business atmosphere. It teaches people to realize that we all have differences. This assessment helps all of us to realize that we all can connect and work as a team. It can be staggering. A guy can be quite surprised to see the scores that confirm he is on the wrong track. They are pretending to be something else when their score says they should be something totally different. In my case, easing up on my dominance was a major step for me, and it made me a better manager. Overall this is one of the best exercises that we could conduct to draw folks together and teach them that everybody has something to offer. You just need to be able to draw that out of the individual, and this focus on communication does that.

A TO Z APPLICATION

1. Are you a good listener? How do you know? _____

   _____

   _____

   _____

2. List someone you know who exemplifies this trait: _____

   _____

   _____

3. On a scale of 1–10, how do you rate on this trait? _____

   _____

   _____

4. What specific things can you do to improve in this area? _____

   _____

   _____

   _____

5. What action *will* you do to improve in this area? _____

   _____

   _____

COMMUNICATION JUMPSTART

- Learn to listen better.
- Learn your DiSC style.
- Turn the cell phone off, leave it in the car, go face to face.
- Respond, don't react. There is a difference.
- Read *Crucial Conversations*—twice!
- Sit, don't stand. It sends the message, "I have time for you."

DECISIVE

It's better to be boldly decisive and risk being wrong than to agonize at length and be right too late. —*Unknown*

de·ci·sive - Having the power to solve or conclude; absolute; characterized by determination and firmness; resolute. / OPPO-SITE - Indecisive; hesitant; suspensive

———

Clients tell me (and research confirms) that one of the most admired traits in a leader is decisiveness. People want those who lead them to be able to make a decision—and stick with it. Ambivalence is confusing, demoralizing, counterproductive, and can even be life threatening. Decisiveness gets things moving; it can help you accomplish great things. After the Chattanooga campaign in the Civil War, General John Rawlins, chief of staff to Ulysses S. Grant, said of Grant, "It is his decisiveness and energy in action that always accomplishes grand results and strikes terror to the hearts of the foe. It is this and not the conception of great schemes that makes military genius."

A decision may not be perfect, but it is far better to execute a good plan in a timely manner than to continue to plan, analyze, and agonize over the 100 percent right decision that gets implemented too late. The Marine Corps calls this the *75 Percent Solution*. They recognize that conditions will never be 100 percent perfect for you to make your decision and execute your plan. In fact, the Marines hold decisiveness as one of the thirteen basic traits of leadership. They define it as the ability to make decisions promptly and to announce them in a clear, forthright manner.

There are different ways to arrive at your decision, many of which will depend on the situation. You might talk to trusted advisers, engage employees, spend time alone, or maybe even flip a coin (not ideal). The stakes and your personal style will influence how you arrive at your final determination, although we do know that better choices are generally made with more complete data, healthy discussion, and sometimes even debate.

The Recognition-Primed Model (RPM) of decision making describes how we make up our minds and what we can do to determine more effective solutions. This matters because a track record of successful decisions instills confidence and improves future decision making. As noted in my earlier book *No Yelling*, it all starts with technical proficiency. The leader has to know and understand what is being attempted. They don't have to be the best at what they supervise but they do need to be familiar with it. When we come upon a situation, we begin to search our mind for previous times we have encountered such a situation. When we find a response that fits the current situation, we take action.

What will you do if you are driving down a busy interstate at 65 MPH and you see brake lights ahead of you in the distance? Most of us would reply along these lines:

1. Ease your foot off the gas.

2. Prepare to step on your brakes.

3. Check the rearview mirror to see if the guy behind you is aware of the situation.

4. Look for a bailout route if you are closing in too fast on the car in front of you.

We can make this reply (which we call an *action script*) because we have been in this situation before, and, therefore, we now know what to do. (Our present actions are determined either because we did them before and they worked for us or because we did something else before and it did *not* work.) It is the same at work and with all decisions. If your action scripts are limited, so will be the quality of your decisions. In fact, in the absence of scripts, you may truly be unable to make a decision.

One of the best things you can do to make better decisions is to expose yourself to situations and scenarios that add to your library of scripts. You can do this for your employees, too. The mind doesn't need to actually *experience the event* to learn the script. Talking about or participating in a simulation is good enough if properly described, discussed, and debriefed. Scenario-based training (SBT) is a term used to describe this higher level effort at enabling leaders to be more decisive.

In fact, SBT has entered the twenty-first century. Timaron Solutions in Greensboro, NC, has created a knowledge transfer process that combines technology, training, and good old-fashioned debriefs. This integrated approach creates leaders who make better decisions and changes organizations into true communities of learning. This learning has a direct payoff in safer, more productive employees who make better decisions. The added benefit of the technology support is the appeal to younger generations who embrace learning from their laptops or other devices.

Here is the deal: If you choose to be a leader, you are being paid for two roles—to make decisions and to get people to act on those decisions. But know this: You *will* make mistakes. That is not a reason to be indecisive. In fact, make the decision, right or wrong, and learn from it (create a new action script). Those you lead will thank you with higher productivity.

The risk of a wrong decision is preferable to the terror of indecision. —Maimonides

DECISIVE IN ACTION

Decisive leadership was determined to be a key success factor during a lessons-learned session held after the successful completion of a very complex project involving a large railroad capacity increase for CSX Transportation. The $220 million design-build project had an extremely tight schedule. The CSX purchase of a large portion of Conrail required double-tracking 120 miles of the old B&O corridor between Chicago and Cleveland to handle the increased freight traffic. A normal schedule for a job like this would have been thirty months. CSX wanted it done in fifteen.

To meet the demanding schedule, Rex Huffman, the project manager for Sverdrup Corporation (now Jacobs Engineering) and the CSX project manager had to be decisive throughout the project execution. There was no time for decisions by committee nor for second-guessing and worrying about making a wrong decision. When the project team had a problem to resolve, a choice to make, or a priority to establish, they gathered rapidly, and decisions were made on the spot. Both of these project managers were empowered by their respective organizations to make critical decisions that might traditionally have been elevated to a higher level. In fact, the project team developed a decision making and resolution escalation hierarchy to ensure decisions were made at the lowest level in the fastest time. Later participants of partnering sessions would quickly recognize this concept, but it was certainly not standard procedure in 1998. It did ensure on-time completion of this project.

Although numerous success factors were identified during the lessons-learned process, Huffman confirms that both management teams agreed that decisiveness was key to the overall project success.

A TO Z APPLICATION

1. On a scale of 1–10, how do you rate on decisiveness? _____

2. With what kind of decisions do you have a hard time? _____

   _____

   _____

3. List someone you know who exemplifies this trait: _____

   _____

4. How well do you conduct after-action reviews to learn from your decisions and make better ones the next time?_____

_____

_____

_____

5. What action *will* you do to improve in this area?_____

_____

_____

DECISIVENESS JUMPSTART

- Embrace imperfection.
- Will the decision you are about to make really matter in five years?
- Get plenty of sleep.
- Create scenarios and "what if" them so when faced with them you will be ready.
- Don't be angry. Angry people make poor decisions.

ENDURANCE

Endurance is one of the most difficult disciplines, but it is to the one who endures that the final victory comes. —*Buddha*

en·dur·ance - The act, quality, or power of withstanding hardship or stress; the state or fact of persevering / OPPOSITE - Fleeting; temporary; transient

———

Leaders set the example, the direction, the pace. Leading requires endurance: physical, mental, and emotional. Let's face it: Not everyone will simply pick up and follow you. Some people might not know how, others may not want to, and still others may not think themselves able. Yet, as a leader, you must create and sustain in all of your followers the belief that they can perform until they can sustain that belief for themselves.

The Marines cite endurance as a leadership trait and define it as mental and physical stamina measured by the ability to withstand pain, fatigue, stress, and hardship. Let's take a look at the physical, mental, and emotional aspects.

Stand at the corner of First and Main in Anytown, USA, and watch people for a while. The irony of the importance of physical balance will become clear: 32.2 percent of American adults are obese—over their ideal weight by at least 20 percent. An additional 30 percent are simply overweight. What does your personal size have to do with your ability to lead? A whole lot, actually. First off, if you stop work due to a physical ailment, you cannot lead. Heart attacks, diabetes, and high blood pressure—directly linked to being overweight—are widespread in our society. But more important, when your body is out of shape, it is simply harder for you to go the distance. The pace and challenges of business have increased greatly in recent years, and keeping up requires greater physical endurance.

Twice a year a client of mine conducts a nine-day corporate university. Three years ago, we added morning activities to the program agenda that entailed some moderate calisthenics followed by a two-mile run or a one-mile walk. The class size is thirty-two. Pretty consistently three or four people can complete the run, and three or four cannot complete the walk. (That's right, *cannot*.) The rest either walk the mile or start off running and reach the finish line walking.

The government reports that more than 40 percent of Americans take at least one prescription drug, and 17 percent take three or more. I am not saying medication is bad; I am saying it means something isn't right in your body. Maybe losing twenty pounds will make the blood pressure go down just as well as the medication would. But a lot of people say they would rather pop a single pill every morning than sweat it out in the gym for an hour every day, even if that would be the more effective treatment in the long run.

When speaking of mental endurance, we recognize that thinking is hard work. We all know people who have declined the chance to step into management. The excuse I hear most often is, "I don't want to do all that paperwork." Sure, some people are better at logic, at thinking things through and seeing the big picture than others. But more are simply giving themselves a pass because they choose not to embrace the challenges of leadership. My question is, "What are you afraid of?"

Sociologist and author Larry Kersten was right when he said, "It's lonely at the top." Just look at the organizational chart. When you're in the top position, there is no one to turn to for help. Who motivates the motivator? It's hard. Leadership is not a popularity contest. People will disagree with you, challenge you, and, on some issues, may fight you outright. It can take an emotional toll on a leader, which underscores the need for developing and maintaining emotional endurance. Without it, you crumble. *Illegitimi non carborundum* is a mock-Latin aphorism meaning "Don't let the bastards grind you down."

Joseph Kennedy said, "When the going gets tough, the tough get going." Make no mistake, leadership is tough. Robert Schuller wrote *Tough Times Never Last, But Tough People Do!* It is a book that is worth your time to read. It is one of the most heavily highlighted, underlined, and marked-up books I own. It had been in a box in the basement for years until I started my research for this book. Schuller wrote, "You won't win if you don't begin." I would add that you will not win if you don't endure.

An important point here is to endure the right things for the right reasons. Simply hanging in there is a waste. Seth Godin in *The Dip* asserts that contrary to Vince Lombardi who told us winners never quit, winners actually quit all the time. They simply know when to quit and when not to quit. He maintains we should "quit the wrong stuff, stick with the right stuff, have the guts to do one or the other." The dip he refers to is the place where we are past beginner and the excitement that comes with beginning but not yet an expert. It can be a long stretch of hard work and frustration. If you are studying to be an engineer, the dip for some happens in calculus.

It did for me, but I knew to quit—after the second time taking the introductory course! Most people don't survive the dip, but the dip is where success is born. It is a crucible that hardens us.

History is replete with examples of people who endured. They stayed in. They persevered and went the distance—Lincoln, Edison, Keller of yesteryear; Hewlett and Packard, Smith, Dell, and Gates of today. Perhaps the most important trait of successful leaders is not that they always succeed but that they respond to setbacks by coming back with a new plan and with renewed vigor.

In October 2004 Hendrick Motor Sports founder, Rick Hendrick, faced a major setback. A plane carrying his management team that included his only son, who was the chosen successor for the business, crashed. There were no survivors. The crash created questions that only Hendrick could answer: Would the business go on? Would they race the next weekend? Eight days after the crash Hendrick stood in front of his employees and told them, "We are going to get through this, and we are going to do it together." This brought his teams together and caused the company to institutionalize succession and contingency planning. Earlier in his life Hendrick had battled leukemia that doctors didn't think he would survive—but he did; he could survive this as well.

Leaders don't surrender. They give that extra effort. When the day is done, they make one more call, do one more task. If the leader doesn't stand tough in the face of obstacles, how can the followers? Endurance must be developed and nourished. Are you getting physical exercise? Is your life in balance? If not, it will be tougher to endure. And your people need that from you. You need it from you, too.

Look back over your career, and you can see the times you had to change. When I speak at conventions, I see people who are embracing change and others who are fighting it. To succeed today means to do things differently than you did them a few years back. I meet executives all the time who have had to remake themselves to remain best positioned to succeed. This doesn't mean they always liked making the change, but longevity in business takes endurance. Adaptability is an integral part of endurance. Simply enduring will wear you down.

At the risk of sounding trite, there are plenty of people who have it worse than you. This is pretty much true no matter where you are in the world. If you are reading this book, you have the time, ability, and desire to get better. Many people in this world cannot read and are oppressed. During the months I was writing this book, two close friends had different but profound accidents. One had a concrete wall fall on him during a mission trip to Haiti. His pelvis was crushed along with a multitude of other serious injuries. Another got struck by a truck driving 50 miles per hour as he ran down the shoulder of a country road. He was in a coma for four weeks then in rehabilitation for another four weeks. The day he came home his wife divorced him. Hang in there. These two guys endured, and they are doing fine today.

On October 29, 1941, UK Prime Minister Winston Churchill visited Harrow School. You are probably familiar with the following portion of his speech: "Never, ever, ever, ever, ever, ever, ever give in. Never give in. Never give in. Never give in." It worked for Sir Winston; it can work for you. On March 3, 1991, Jim Valvano, his body racked with cancer, spoke at the first ESPY awards in Madison Square Garden. He created the Jimmy V Foundation for Cancer Research and gave it the motto: "Don't give up, don't ever give up."

When the going gets tough, that's when we like it. —*Knute Rockne*

ENDURANCE IN ACTION

When Brian was a teenager, he spent his summers working at construction sites as an apprentice. He enjoyed the work, but after high school he went to Massachusetts Maritime Academy where he graduated with a degree in Marine engineering.

After graduation Brian decided to pursue a career outside of construction. However, through this time Brian felt something was missing in his life. He missed the challenges that came with each and every home improvement project. And he truly missed the satisfaction he knew his work brought to his clients. To fulfill this emptiness, Brian continued to work at his full-time job, but he also started taking on after-hours remodeling projects. With satisfied clients came more work. After a few years of working long days, seven days a week, his construction business started to flourish. Brian took the risk to turn his passion into a full-time career, and in 1999 Neponset Valley Construction (NVC) was launched.

Neponset Valley Construction is a full-service residential and commercial building, remodeling, and renovation company located in Norwood, Massachusetts. Brian has worked diligently to have NVC become one of the most trusted names in quality workmanship. Through steady leadership, hard work, and endurance, Neponset Valley Construction grew and was recently awarded "2010 Best of Boston Home." He also received a Super Service Award from Angie's List (a site that more than one million consumers visit looking for quality contractors).

Simply stated, Brian endured and persevered. Certainly there were challenges along the way—from the initial decision to step into business ownership to the need to adapt his product offering along with client demands and building technology. Brian Kearney, Neponset Valley's owner says, "There's something to be said for a company that has been able not only to survive but also to grow in this economy." That something is endurance.

A TO Z APPLICATION

1. On a scale of 1–10, how do you rate on endurance? _____

2. Listen to the Valvano speech on Youtube.

3. Be honest—what kind of shape is your body in? _____

   _____

   _____

   _____

4. What changes have you made to enable you to endure? How have you adapted to stay at the top of your game? _____

   _____

   _____

   _____

5. What specific things can you do to improve in this area? _____

   _____

   _____

   _____

ENDURANCE JUMPSTART

- Read *Tough Times Never Last, But Tough People Do*.
- Develop a support network. For example, I have a personal board of directors.
- Develop and maintain your sense of humor.
- Read *The Dip*.
- Don't quit.

FAIR

Fairness is man's ability to rise above his prejudices. —*Wes Fessler*

fair - Free from bias, dishonesty, or injustice / OPPOSITE - Below the belt; cheating; partial; unjust

———

It has been said that life isn't fair, and this may well be true. But when it comes to leadership, you must be fair. Your people expect it. And when they get it, they respond with enthusiasm that increases production and reduces defects.

This is not to say that all situations and all people must be treated equally. But they must be treated equitably—fairly. Different situations call for different solutions. It is impossible—not to mention ineffective—to apply the same solutions to similar problems when different personalities are involved. People recognize this and accept it, as long as you are fair when you do it. If you are not fair, they will think you are playing favorites and will either perform at a low level or leave you altogether. In fact, on the opposite spectrum of enthusiasm is another emotional state called anger. Anger stems from injustice or unfair treatment.

Once again, my colleagues in the Marines recognize fairness as an essential leadership trait. Though they use the word justice, the concept remains the same: giving reward or punishment according to the merits of the case in question. Donald Pfaff and Edward Wilson wrote in *The Neuroscience of Fair Play: Why We (Usually) Follow the Golden Rule* that human beings are naturally programmed to treat one another in a civil, thoughtful manner. "As employees we are drawn to companies that do so." We become emotionally attached to companies (as employees and as customers) that practice this principle and treat us as real people when they make decisions.

Let me give you an example. Employee A has been coming to work late. So has Employee B. If you choose to apply equal treatment to each of them and you have a "three strikes" rule, then once they both are late three times, you must fire both of them. That is equal treatment. But let's go a bit deeper. Employee A is a long-ball hitter for you. She takes on the tough assignments and performs superbly. Her school-age child has been sick with a prolonged bout of the flu that has caused her to be late several times. On the days she arrives late, she stays later to catch up on her work or she takes it home with her. Employee B has no mitigating circumstances. She comes to work late, has no excuse, and is the first one to hit the door at quitting time. Now tell me what is fair?

Equal treatment says fire them both; fair treatment says you take care of Employee A. Now, several months later, employee C is coming to work late. Her mother was just admitted to a nursing home, and C visits her every morning to help make the transition smoother. She is not a long-ball hitter, but she gets her work done in a satisfactory manner. She, too, stays late or takes work home to get it done. If you don't make the same accommodation for her that you made for employee A, you are acting unfairly. And in acting unfairly, you turn off the members of your workforce who see what's going on. (And be assured, they do see it—and talk about it.)

In *The Enthusiastic Employee: How Companies Profit by Giving Workers What They Want*, the authors address thirty-three common myths about employees. One widely held belief they tackle is what employees want at work. The overwhelming majority of workers are shown to have three main goals at work: equity, achievement, and camaraderie. Let's look more closely at equity. The authors define it as being treated justly in relation to the basic conditions of employment (especially physical safety, pay, benefits, job security, and respectful treatment). Again we see the concept of fairness front and center. This sentiment is reinforced by Kouzes and Posner in

The Leadership Challenge, where fair-mindedness was in the top five most-admired leadership characteristics. We can concisely summarize the data on fairness by saying that adults want to be treated as adults on a team where everyone has the same opportunity to excel. Simply stated: It is an issue of respect.

The Corporate Leavers Survey conducted by the Level Playing Field Institute in January 2007 shows that each year in this country, more than two million professionals and managers leave their jobs, pushed out by cumulative small comments, whispered jokes, and not-so-funny e-mail. This study, the first large-scale review of this issue, shows that unfairness costs U.S. employers $64 billion *annually*. Notice this survey only addresses managers; it doesn't even consider production employees.

Be consistent (not equal) in how you handle situations. Make accommodations that you can justify. And through it all, recognize that the performance standard has not changed. If people are not getting their work done correctly, then you must take corrective action. But when you earn a reputation as being a fair boss, you earn the loyalty of your employees—and that helps your bottom line.

It is not fair to ask of others what you are unwilling to do yourself.
—Eleanor Roosevelt

FAIRNESS IN ACTION

I had just taken over as the regional manager in my company. My leadership style was very different from the fellow I replaced and it was an adjustment period for all. I tended to be hands off while the guy before me tended to get in the middle of everything. He was involved in all aspects of the operation, and all disputes went through him. My first take on a dispute is for people to work it out like adults. If they cannot do that, I then expect them to come to me with solutions rather than for me simply to referee.

Linda in sales and Karyn in estimating were not getting along. They didn't respect each other, and it seemed they were trying to make each other look bad. This was a situation for me to be hands on. I called them both in and told them what I was seeing and what I expected. I clearly explained their behavior was immature and not acceptable. I even got each of them some one-on-one coaching to help them understand themselves and each other.

Unfortunately the situation didn't get better, and I put them both on notice that if they continued to bicker, one of them would be moved. Around this time they both had some personal issues with family health that caused them to miss work at inconvenient hours. Initially they both got their work done, but after a few weeks

Linda was not making her sales targets. She simply was not making the calls she needed to make to meet her sales targets. Karyn continued to be absent from time to time, but her work never suffered. In fact, she was absent more than Linda, but her work was fine. Their relationship remained unproductive although they were seeing each other less.

Finally it was time for a counseling session with Linda. Despite allowances I made for her absences, her performance was not up to standard. I laid out the problem as I saw it, and she immediately chose to use a diversionary tactic by pointing out that Karyn was taking extra time off, too. I replied that this was not about Karyn. Linda replied that it was not fair that Karyn was allowed to take more time and that she was not being called to task for it. I reminded her that this was not about Karyn but then went on to say that Karyn continued to get her work done even with the extra time she was taking off. I told Linda she was free to take as much time as she needed, but the issue was about her productivity. She committed to getting back on track, but she never did. She continued to be distracted at home and continued to point out what Karyn was doing wrong. Her home situation got better, and I hoped for improvement.

A few weeks later, I let Linda go. She protested that it was not fair, failing to recognize her lack of production as the cause for her termination. She said I was not treating them the same, that if she was going to be fired that Karyn needed to be fired, too. She didn't get it. In fact, she lodged a complaint with the EEOC that we then had to defend. The case was dismissed. Karyn eventually came back to work full time and was very appreciative of the support I had given her.

Several weeks later an employee who had only been with us for six months faced similar issues at home. He needed time, but he didn't have any vacation time to use nor had he established the credibility over time that Karyn and Linda had to justify any real accommodation. I gave him similar, though not quite as liberal, latitude in scheduling his hours. Fortunately the situation at home was resolved in a few weeks and he was back at work. Several months later, at his annual review, he told me he was grateful for the way I had treated him. He didn't expect that and had made up his mind to quit so that he could be with his wife. He told me he would never forget, and if I needed anything special to make sure I called on him. He is one of our future stars, and we would have lost him had I not treated him fairly.

A TO Z APPLICATION

1. On a scale of 1–10, how do you rate on this trait? _____

2. Do you have "go to" people on your team? What message does this send to others? _____

   _____

   _____

   _____

3. Who is someone you know who exemplifies this trait? _____

   _____

4. Do you extend the same basic courtesies (hello, good morning, how are you, etc.) to *all* the people on your team? _____

   _____

   _____

5. What action *will* you do to improve in this area? _____

   _____

   _____

   _____

FAIRNESS JUMPSTART

- Don't play favorites.
- Go above the law. Harassment and discrimination, no matter how subtle, must be addressed.
- Think how your decisions impact all of your employees.
- Be aware if you spend more time with some employees than with others, and manage the situation.
- Read *The Enthusiastic Employee*.

GENUINE

Never idealize others. They will never live up to your expectations. Don't overanalyze your relationships. Stop playing games. A growing relationship can only be nurtured by genuineness. —Leo F. Buscaglia

gen·u·ine - Free from pretense, affectation, or hypocrisy; sincere; not counterfeit; authentic; real / OPPOSITE - False; pretended; fake; phony; inauthentic

———

Leadership is fundamentally about people. People want to work for those they trust and those they know will take care of them. People want to work for you (or not). **Being genuine is about being the real you.** In my world of professional speaking, this applies when the person you see on the stage bears little resemblance to the one you meet in the lobby. They may talk of grace and respect on stage but then act like jerks offstage. At best they might be a good actor, but at worst they are simply phony.

Authentic is another word to describe this concept of what you see is what you get and, more important, what is really there in the first place. If you are tough and demanding, then be that way. If you are warm and effusive, then be that way. Whatever you are, be that and no more. People have an innate ability to know when you are not being straight with them. People get that gut feeling and know when you are insincere. They will be off balance when they don't know which "you" is going to show up to work. Will it be the Dr. Jekyll or the Mr. Hyde? Off-balance people don't perform well. In fact, keep them off balance enough, and they will leave.

Authenticity is a technical term in existentialist philosophy. It is the degree to which one is true to one's own personality, spirit, or character. To go any further with this line of thought would get us deep into philosophy with the likes of Sartre, Fromm, and Descartes, and we are not going there!

We are all human, and that brings fragile hopes, complicated emotions, and heavy baggage from years gone by. There is no escaping being human. Actually, being genuine is all about embracing your humanity—not escaping it. That doesn't mean bad behavior and false pretenses are condoned. It does mean you are okay with who you are, and you work to be a better you. Alcoholics Anonymous exhorts its members to claim spiritual progress, not perfection, because they know the push for perfection is the sure path to disappointment and, for them, alcohol abuse.

The push for progress recognizes you are a work in progress. Noted golf coach Bob Rotella wrote a book titled *Golf Is Not a Game of Perfect*. I would add, neither is life nor leadership. He states this doesn't mean professional golfers don't strive to eliminate mistakes from their game. But the pro also understands that while striving for perfection is essential, demanding perfection on the golf course is deadly. As with the golf pro, when you start accepting yourself, you open yourself to relationships, support, and opportunities you would not otherwise have gotten.

I sometimes hesitate to tell people I am a professional speaker. There are a lot of speakers out there who are not genuine. They stand in front of you and tell you one thing and live a life contrary to that when they are offstage. How can you speak on leadership when you have never actually led anything? And what about the fitness and nutrition coach who is overweight? Not a lot of credibility there. They aren't being real with you, and, deep down, you don't trust them.

Bill George, author of *True North*, wrote, "What, then, is the twenty-first-century leader all about? It is being authentic, uniquely yourself, the genuine article. Authentic leaders know who they are. They are 'good in their skin,' so good they don't feel a need to impress or please others." He tells us that when you are true to who you are, you can cope with the most difficult circumstances that life presents. When you are aligned with who you are, you find coherence between your life story and your leadership. When you feel in the zone and are filled with supreme confidence, you have found what he calls True North. When you are aligned with your True North, you are ready to lead others authentically.

Leaders who are genuine can have a bad day and not worry about losing their game face. If you are consistently you, your people have the assurance and comfort of knowing what to expect and wanting to excel. If you are inconsistent, they will hold back.

Go ahead, be yourself, really. It's okay.

No one man can, for any considerable time, wear one face to himself, and another to the multitude, without finally getting bewildered as to which is the true one. —Hawthorne

GENUINE IN ACTION

W. E. O'Neil Construction is an ENR Top 200 general contractor with offices in Illinois, Colorado, California, and Arizona. Much of their work is negotiated with repeat clients. The depth and quality of these client relationships are an essential element of their ongoing success. A recent project interview with a new client presented an opportunity for a young project manager to simply be himself. Listen to Brad Fry, director of personnel development at O'Neil, tell it:

> It is common for an owner to schedule interviews with two or three low bidders prior to awarding a contract for work. One of the primary goals of the meeting is to evaluate the staff assigned to the project. We had one such interview with an owner we had not previously worked with and were presenting a young project manager (Joel) together with an experienced superintendent. Not surprisingly, the experienced superintendent needed to say only a few sentences about his approach to the work to gain the owner's trust and confidence. The young project manager, however, was not so warmly accepted, due largely to his age.
>
> When the owner asked Joel how many times he had worked with this particular superintendent, he replied confidently, "Twice." Unfortunately, while explaining the first occasion, Joel realized he had actually only worked with this fellow once. Since the owner had asked him to explain the first occasion in detail, Joel correctly anticipated the next question: Can you tell us about the second experience? True to our corporate values, Joel admitted the

truth—there had only been one previous project together. But rather than stop there, he added, "I must have been thinking of the book club." Joel explained that the company sponsored a book club wherein a title was selected and advertised to the employees. Anyone expressing interest was given the book and asked to join in a discussion at lunch one day. The superintendent in question had been to a book club meeting that he had also attended.

When the owner called to award us the job, he mentioned the book club and how impressed he was that a company would do such a thing. While none of us believe that we got the job because of the book club, it sure made an impression. Fortunately we'll never know what might have happened had Joel tried to cover up his error by inventing a phantom experience with the superintendent. We'll also never know what might have happened if Joel hadn't decided to be himself and to take a shot at explaining the book club to a prospective client.

A TO Z APPLICATION

1. On a scale of 1–10, how do you rate on this trait? _____

2. Are you consistent at work and at home? _____

3. List someone you know who exemplifies this trait: _____

   _____

4. About what do you pretend? What don't you want people to
   know about you? _____

   _____

   _____

5. What action *will* you do to improve in this area?_____

   _____

   _____

GENUINE JUMPSTART

- Read *How To Win Friends and Influence People.*
- Learn how to be assertive, not aggressive.
- Accept yourself—life is not a game of perfect.
- Communicate in person with people. It is tough to be genuine in a text message.
- Do your best and be pleased with the outcome.

While these heroic leaders do deliver results, research and wisdom tell us there is a better way. Some would call it servant leadership. The term *servant leadership* was coined by Robert Greenleaf in 1970. The Greenleaf website tells us, "The servant-leader *is* servant first. It begins with the natural feeling that one wants to serve, to serve *first*. Then conscious choice brings one to aspire to lead. That person is sharply different from one who is *leader* first . . . The leader-first and the servant-first are two extreme types."

As out of place as that might seem in the twenty-first century, recent research uncovered the fact that, despite the power we associate with the idea of leader, 93 percent of those who actually lead an organization view themselves at least partially as a servant of the people they lead. As human beings, none of us is "better" than another. Others may do certain things better, but that doesn't make them better as people. Someone may occupy a different station in life—or position in the company—but that doesn't increase or lessen their value. The caste system in India was predicated on the belief that some people simply came into the world with more value, while others were born inferior. But here in the United States, even being the CEO of the corporation doesn't make someone "better." They may have more responsibility, but they don't have more worth as a human being. And wise leaders understand the important and dynamic relationship they have with those who follow them.

HUMBLE

*To be humble to superiors is duty, to equals courtesy, to inferiors noble-
ness.* —Benjamin Franklin

hum·ble - Not arrogant; modest; courteously respectful / OPPO-
SITE - Arrogant; stuck-up; disdainful; egotistical; hubris

———

In our society the words *humble* and *leader* don't often go together.
Put them side by side, and you get an oxymoron—you know, two
things that don't go together, like jumbo shrimp or aluminum
armor. The concept of the *heroic* leader is far more consistent with
conventional wisdom on leadership. But it is far less effective today
than in earlier times. Heroic leaders are those larger-than-life figures
who stand above the organization urging it forward. Moses would
certainly be in this category. Contemporary business might look at
Jack Welch as a heroic leader of the late twentieth century.

Jim Collins describes the level five leader in *Good to Great*. The humble leader works to surround himself with smart people. When you have that celebrity leader, you get "one genius with 1000 helpers." The level five leader puts the company first. Celebrities put themselves first. People don't support the boss who does this. There is a direct relationship between the absence of celebrity and the presence of good-to-great results. When Starbucks founder Howard Schultz returned to the CEO role, he was forced to look at the missteps that had weakened the company. He also emphasized doing things right to make it better. He could have cut health care, but that would have been a violation of trust. When facing cutbacks, he conducted a company-wide meeting. He recalls "people went after me. I stood there and answered the questions, and I apologized for making decisions that people thought fractured the trust we had built for so many years." He goes on to talk about leaders celebrating the human connection and to make sure people realize the deep level of respect for the work they do and how they act.

Marine Corps history serves us well here. Major General John A. Lejeune, the commandant of the Marine Corps from 1920–1929, writes, "The relationship between officers and enlisted should in no sense be that of superior and inferior, nor that of master and servant, but that of teacher and scholar." I have always liked that quote. I remember reading it in a recruiting booklet when I was in high school. I still like it. If you are a leader, you would do well to like it too.

The problem with some leaders stems from the perks and privileges accrued by the leader. In my work with senior leaders, I've stayed at plush resorts and flown on corporate jets. It's pretty heady stuff that can lead to arrogance and a false sense of entitlement. It's interesting to note that hubris, or excessive pride, was actually a crime on par with treason in the sixth century BC. In that same era, King Solomon cautioned his men, "It is not good to seek one's own honor. Doing so is like eating too much honey. Sweet as it is, and healthy as it is in proper amounts, too much of this good thing will make you sick—and sick of it."

Several years ago I invited a number of smart, talented people to join me in Raleigh for what could best be called the first FireStarter Corporate meeting. At the time, each of these people served as subcontractors to my firm, some on a very regular basis and some only occasionally. Each was an accomplished professional and highly regarded in his or her field. They didn't *need* to be in Raleigh. They could have been anywhere. But they chose to be with me. When I led Marines, I may have been leading an all-volunteer force, but beyond that these people *didn't* choose me. When I led in business, the supervisors *didn't* choose me; they chose the company I worked for. But this time in Raleigh, these people *chose* to follow me. It was one of the most humbling experiences of my life.

The age of the heroic leader is over. This fallacy was perpetuated in the CEO-as-media-icon days of the late 1990s. It was wrong then, and it's wrong now. While there are instances of successful leaders of the heroic model, the greater truth is that *the most successful leaders recognize **the privilege of leadership** and are humbled by the opportunity to serve.* Humility has been defined as a clear recognition of what and who we really are, followed by a sincere attempt to become what we can be. *Humble* doesn't brag about itself; it simply acts with honesty and tolerance. *Humble* wins.

If I have seen further than others, it is by standing upon the shoulders of giants. —Isaac Newton

HUMILITY IN ACTION

It would be contrary to the entire concept of humility to single out any one person here. It would probably bother them if I were to do so. However, the principle remains. To respect the people I place in this category, I will illustrate some of the behaviors that put them here.

Opening doors for someone may seem like an antiquated gesture, but for a regional vice president I know well it underscores his belief that he is part of the team. This isn't just any region for just any company. It is half the United States for one of the largest contractors in the world.

Listening skills are a key part of communication, but, done well, they also send the message to other people that they matter. I know a senior leader who makes you feel like the most important person in the world while you are talking with him. He asks for your point of view and considers it deeply before commenting thoughtfully on it. He has an open mind that is based on his humility that he does not have all the answers.

I learned in the Marines to eat last. It meant my people were taken care of. I see precious few leaders practice this in the civilian sector. They are often in the front of the line at the lunch buffet and care little if there is nothing left when the last employees come through. I work with a vice president of human resources who always goes last in the buffet line. He checks to see what is being served and then goes to the end of the line. It seems like such a little thing, but it is always noticed by students in training.

A regional manager I know will pick up debris as he walks a job. Cleanliness is a priority for this subcontractor doing high process work. He not only sets an example, but he shows everyone that no one is above keeping the jobsite clean. When I walk with him, I have learned to pick up debris too.

A TO Z APPLICATION

1. On a scale of 1–10, how do you rate on this trait? _____

2. Do you equate humble with timid? _____
   _____

3. List someone you know who exemplifies this trait: _____
   _____

4. Try saying, "You were right" more often.

5. Do you eat last? _____

6. What action *will* you do to improve in this area? _____
   _____
   _____

HUMILITY JUMPSTART

- Remember, the next person you meet is important, and you might learn something from him or her.
- Do volunteer work; support causes you believe in.
- Learn to apologize. Saying, "I was wrong" will not kill you. Say it. "My bad" doesn't cut it.
- Read most anything by His Holiness the Dalai Lama.

INTEGRITY

Trust is the great simplifier. If people in business told the truth, 80 to 90 percent of their problems would disappear. —*Will Schutz*

in·teg·ri·ty - Steadfast adherence to a strict moral or ethical code; the state of being unimpaired; soundness; / OPPOSITE - Unethical; liar; unsound; immoral

———

No surprise here: If people can't trust you, they will not want to follow you. The only reason some folks *might* follow you is out of mild curiosity—so they can witness the train wreck your career becomes when your lack of honesty, accountability, and decency catch up with you.

When we see the word *integrity*, most of us think of honesty, of being truthful. The *Stanford Encyclopedia of Philosophy* tells us, "Integrity is one of the most important and oft-cited of virtue terms.

It is also perhaps the most puzzling. For example, while it is sometimes used virtually synonymously with 'moral,' we also, at times, distinguish acting morally from acting with integrity. Persons of integrity may in fact act immorally." A thief or liar could tell you they are a thief or a liar and act as one, and they would be acting with integrity but perhaps immorally. The Marine Corps addresses this by defining integrity as uprightness of character and soundness of moral principles, including the qualities of truthfulness and honesty. The fact that integrity enters the realm of philosophy means we are in for something complex.

Let's look at the facets of integrity that relate to leading. Think about the values you stress to your employees. They may include efficiency, teamwork, or service. Do you say a certain procedure is the *right way* to do things at your place (because it supports those values)? Then do you not hold someone accountable if they deviate from that procedure? Although it may not strictly fit the definition, at root this is an integrity issue: You say one thing but do another. Have you ever told someone you would call them back, and then didn't? Do it once and they may forgive you. Do it twice, and you have an integrity issue because you are no longer perceived as truthful.

Research continues to underscore this key trait. Jim Kouzes and Larry Posner, in *The Leadership Challenge*, cite honesty as *the most important supervisory trait* in every study they have done since 1981. Over the years, no fewer than 87 percent of respondents listed honesty as the quality they value most in a superior. In my earlier book, *No Yelling, The 9 Secrets of Marine Corps Leadership You Must Know to Win in Business*, integrity is such an important topic that the entire first chapter is dedicated to it. Everyone I interviewed for the book cited integrity as an essential element of leadership.

How often have you seen a manager deliver a message to workers and say, "I don't agree with it, but Corporate told us we have to do it"? What about the manager who decides to fire someone and blames it on cutbacks? And then there is the performance review where the manager says everything is "fine" but fails to address a critical performance issue with the employee. In each case, the manager is evading the truth and acting without integrity. His people will have little faith in him and little respect for him as a supervisor. This, in turn, will make him a weak and ineffective leader.

The recent excesses and abuses on Wall Street make this topic even more important. In the face of such reckless behavior, how is a leader to stand fast and act with integrity? David Callahan, author of *The Cheating Culture*, asserts that cheating is on the rise and there are four reasons for this: new pressures, bigger rewards for winning, temptation, and trickle-down corruption. Four reasons to cheat.

One reason not to: We all know it is wrong. Wrong gets you into trouble. Legendary Penn State football coach Joe Paterno puts it this way, "Whether you are on a sports team, in an office, or a member of a family, if you can't trust one another there is going to be trouble."

Tony Simons, author of *The Integrity Dividend*, proclaims that integrity is worth it. His website opens by saying, "Your effectiveness in relationships depends on how much people see you as living by your word. Where they see it strongly, people trust you more, listen more closely to you, and allow you to influence them. This form of credibility is necessary to lead, to sell, and to address conflicts. It shows up on the bottom line as the integrity dividend." I guess it wouldn't surprise you that His Holiness the Dalai Lama thinks highly of honesty, "I think humans and animals have an innate appreciation for truth. If we treat dogs and cats sincerely, they appreciate it. If we cheat them they realize it and don't like it. If one human being communicates truthfully with another it will be appreciated. If we cheat others, they will react accordingly whether they are believers or nonbelievers, rich or poor, educated or uneducated."

Before you can move on from this chapter, you must focus inward. The most important person with whom you must be honest is yourself. It all flows from there. We talked about this a bit when we discussed the quality of being genuine, but we must revisit it here. Motivational speaker Jim Jackson says, "Honesty is a value we all cherish." To get honesty from others, we must first give it to ourselves. To the golfers among my readers, I ask, "What is your handicap? Your real one. Do you ever take a mulligan or a gimme putt?" We all do sometimes. But listen to the old gent from Scotland when the Yank walked off 18 saying, "I shot a 79 with only one mulligan." The Scot replied, "Ah, laddie, here that would be an 81." What is your real golf handicap?

When people think of you, do they think of someone with integrity? Why don't you ask them?

If you tell the truth you don't have to remember anything. —Mark Twain

INTEGRITY IN ACTION

A regional paving company, which was part of an international infrastructure firm, negotiated with a national retailer to provide a quote for a substantial project involving dirt work, providing mix, guardrails, sewer/utilities, paving, and some other miscellaneous work for a new supercenter. The bid process took several months, during which the project manager reviewed the specifications for the work to be quoted and had numerous meetings (via telephone and face-to-face) with various representatives from the retailer. After submitting a total quote of $1,500,000 (lump sum contract), the firm was awarded the work, and the owner wrote up the contract. The location of the job enabled the contractor to provide a competitive bid based on logistics, and they anticipated a handsome profit.

As the job progressed, the project manager realized there was a portion of dirt work and paving that was listed in the quote that was not being done. No one from the retailer raised any issues or concerns, and all work to date had been acceptable. The project manager went back and reviewed the final signed contract. He discovered the contract, which was prepared by the legal team for the retailer and found that did not include the area in question in the portion of the contract entitled "Work to Be Completed." The project manager checked his notes from initial meetings with representatives from the retailer, the initial specifications and his original written quote all confirmed that the dirt work and paving in that area should have been completed, but the owner had omitted it from the contract. The lump sum amount had not changed.

The project manager immediately brought this to the attention of the regional manager. Despite the inclusion of the area in the initial conversations, it was not listed on the final contract, and the contractor stood to make extra money on the job since it was a lump sum contract. This was clearly an oversight by the legal team for the retailer. The contractor had no legal obligation to do the work or even to raise the issue. However, the bigger question was what was the right thing to do? The contractor prided himself on taking care of the customer and dealing with integrity with all parties. This was explicitly stated in its corporate values. Still, this was also an opportunity to make an extra 10 percent on the job.

The project manager and the regional manager quickly agreed that the right thing to do was to contact the retailer and point out the oversight. Of course, the retailer appreciated the candor and integrity of the project team. As a result of their action, they were asked to bid on several other jobs the retailer was doing in the region, and sister companies of this subsidiary were introduced to the other regional construction teams for the retailer.

The contractor believes doing the right thing in the right way is the only way to do business. The project manager behaved in accordance with that belief, and the owner and the firm benefited in the long run.

A TO Z APPLICATION

1. On a scale of 1–10, how do you rate on this trait? _____

2. When is the last time you told a little white lie? _____

_____

_____

3. List someone you know who exemplifies this trait. What do they do that is exemplary? _____

_____

4. Do you consistently live up to your commitments? Ask those you trust if you do. _____

_____

5. What action *will* you do to improve in this area?_____

_____

_____

INTEGRITY JUMPSTART

- Deliver on your commitments.
- Play by the rules.
- Understand why and when you lie.
- Read *Integrity: The Courage to Meet the Demands of Reality.*
- Read *Winners Never Cheat.*

JUDGMENT

Reason and judgment are the qualities of a leader. —*Tacitus*

judg·ment - The ability to make a decision or form an opinion objectively, authoritatively, and wisely, esp. in matters affecting action; good sense; discretion

———

This chapter was one of the toughest to write. In researching the topic, I found plenty of material on the Last Judgment and business judgment in the legal sense. I learned that a deck of tarot cards has a judgment card, and when this card appears in a "reading," it is usually interpreted as a sign of an impending decision. But in business there are no tarot card readings (or at least, very few). Yet a leader must exercise sound judgment. The question is, how? Noted academics Noel Tichy and Warren Bennis have written a book called *Judgment: How Winning Leaders Make Great Calls.* They make the important point that judgment is a skill that can be developed, refined, and nurtured.

Let's refer back to the dictionary definition that we started with. Judgment is the ability to form an opinion objectively, authoritatively, and wisely. The leader must be able to take in data from multiple sources and give it all a fair hearing. These data sources may be conflicting. You may not personally like someone who is giving you information, but you still need to take it in. Good judgment means suspending belief in one particular course of action and *objectively* (that is, in an unbiased manner) assessing all others.

In being authoritative, we see the leader delivering judgment with confidence and conviction. Once the decision is made, they issue it forcefully and without doubt. If a leader relates to his team a plan he came up with on the way to work that he thinks might save the company (and their jobs) but adds, "It probably won't work," is he demonstrating good judgment? Of course not. I would suggest that judgment is first about *thinking* and second about *doing*. It also improves with your communication skills. The problem for a lot of managers is that they communicate poorly and would rather *do* than *think*. They wrongly believe that getting the job done is the most important thing.

"Remember, I pay you for your judgment." I still remember these words from the first CEO I worked for after my time in the

Marines. He was explaining to me that I was not going to be simply the technical expert; I would be supervising people who had been doing the job a long time. I would be among peers who had a higher level of expertise. And he told me that I would not be in that job forever. But, while I was there, he expected me to learn and to make good decisions based on the information I had and on the guidance he gave me. He wasn't paying me for my ability to do work; he wasn't paying me for my education. He wasn't even paying me for my experience in the Marines. He was paying me for my *ability to pull together all those assets and make a sound decision*.

In *Getting It Right: Notre Dame on Leadership and Judgment in Business* by Viva Bartkus and Ed Conlon, we see "Business is really about performance in the end, and performance is around your judgment, and judgment in the end rests on your values." While judgment may rest on your values, where does it come from? My CEO paid me for it, but where did I get it? For this discussion, we can say that judgment comes from two places—*experience* and *intuition*. In some cases, experience feeds intuition, but I am keeping them apart to make the discussion clearer.

Experience is the "been there, done that, got the T-shirt and don't want to do it again" perspective that causes me to not repeatedly touch a hot stove. Yes, it's a great teacher, but it can also be a very costly one. As a leader, you should create learning opportunities for your people so they can gain experience. You should also seek to learn from the experience of others. Get them to give you the T-shirt so you don't have to go through the hassle of getting it yourself.

Intuition has long been viewed as involving a form of analyzing information that differs from rational or analytical processes. Distinctions between "rational" and "nonrational" human thought can be traced as far back as Aristotle. The key point is that intuition is a subconscious activity, while most of us would view judgment at the conscious level. In fact, recent research using functional MRIs and other new technologies tells us our emotions, or "gut," play a much bigger factor in decision making than we ever thought. It is tough to disentangle them and far easier to accept and admit the importance of the rational *and* the nonrational in solid judgment. The key for the leader is not only to allow but also to *encourage* both levels of thought to function and to pay attention to both when making decisions.

Amar Bhide, Tufts University professor of business, asserts super computers and analytical models have reduced our capacity for judgment in a time when we need it most. The pace of the twenty-first century can be described as hyper. In moments, perhaps seconds, information cannot be fully passed to a centralized planner using a computer program. And in that delay an opportunity has passed. Decentralization is based on the judgment of the individual at the point of action. Individuals with knowledge of what is happening at a given place in time must be given the latitude to make a timely decision. It might be nice if algorithms and calculations could make all our decisions, but they cannot. Remember that leadership is about *people*, *relationships*, and *performance*. Decisions in these areas simply cannot be automated.

How about you? What are you paid for? What are you paying your managers to do? Are they doers? Thinkers? You get paid for your judgment. How good is it?

A hasty judgment is a first step to recantation. —*Publilius Syrus*

JUDGMENT IN ACTION

Vince was the new (external hire) president for a $100 million subsidiary of a national highway construction company. The subsidiary had operated in this top thirty American city for over thirty years, and the outgoing president had been a fixture in the city. However, the firm had seen several years of declining sales and profits. The incumbent president chose to rest on his laurels, but the negative trend necessitated a change in leadership.

Upon his arrival, Vince did all the things that good leaders do. He met his team, he learned the business, he learned the market, and he listened a lot. He took a close look outside the walls of his company to fully understand the dynamics of the market. He was disturbed by what he saw, but the facts were impossible to ignore. Over time, the once invincible construction firm had lost its market leadership position. In fact, growth by competitors had actually put the firm at a competitive disadvantage in the market. This disadvantage was clearly illustrated by the deteriorating financial performance.

The parent firm had a very successful track record of growth in North America through organic means and through acquisition. They were adept at scouting for good deals. Their philosophy was to buy and hold. In fact, they had never divested a company. Yet this was exactly what Vince was suggesting. He had done the internal and external analysis and presented his opinion. In his judgment, the firm should be sold. In effect, he was eliminating his job, but he knew it was the right thing to do. He was initially rebuffed. That simply wasn't their way. But in the next few months, as financials continued to be poor, he continued to explain his thought process. Despite applying all the best practices of leadership and management he could, the firm continued to lose money. Based on his recommendation, the company was put up for sale.

A bidding war quickly ensued from two of the market leaders. In fact, the logical firm to make the acquisition based on size and existing market position was being outbid by a smaller firm looking to make a bigger impact in the market. The problem was the CEO of this smaller purchasing firm got his ego in the process, and he failed to do the analysis for the real value of what he was purchasing. He didn't really understand the market dynamics. The larger firm backed out of the bidding, and the smaller winning bidder gloated about his business acumen.

Unfortunately for him, he paid too much for assets that were not positioned well in the market. Just over two years after the acquisition, the firm was virtually insolvent and forced to sell at a discount. In this case, the CEO exercised poor judgment, and the subsequent collapse of his company confirmed it.

A TO Z APPLICATION

1. On a scale of 1–10, how do you rate on judgment? _____

2. How would you like to be described by people? _____

   _____

   _____

   _____

3. List someone you know who exemplifies sound judgment: __

   _____

   _____

4. Which emotions drive your judgment? _____

_____

_____

_____

5. What action *will* you do to improve in this area? _____

_____

_____

_____

JUDGMENT JUMPSTART

- Conduct after-action reviews to determine what went right and wrong and to learn for next time.
- Have mentors to learn from.
- Read *Judgment: How Winning Leaders Make Great Calls*
- Evaluate every decision and action as it would be reported on the front page of a newspaper.

KNOWLEDGEABLE

Information is not knowledge. —*Albert Einstein*

knowl·edge·a·ble - Possessing or exhibiting knowledge; insight; intelligent; well-informed; discerning; perceptive / OPPOSITE - Uneducated; uninformed; ignorant

———

There is a high expectation that the leader be competent in the assigned task or specialty he or she is supervising. This expectation exists at some level in all endeavors. Workers want the boss to know what they do and to have, at least, a rudimentary understanding of how it is done. At a minimum, the leader should be familiar with the task. Even better, he or she should have some proficiency at it.

Bank of America CEO Brian Moynihan "knows his stuff soup to nuts, and expects you to know your stuff also," says Anne Finucane, BofA's global strategy and marketing officer, who has worked with Moynihan for about 15 years. Compare that to the classic CEO as founder who begins to lose control of the business because he doesn't have a broader knowledge base on which to build. Research by Harvard professor Noam Wasserman shows that the percentage of founder-CEOs who "go the distance" is extremely low, especially in high-potential ventures. People like Bill Gates and Larry Ellison, who are able to lead their companies for quite a while, get all the attention because they are rare, not because they are typical. The importance of this trait is not limited to business. NFL receiver and Peyton Manning's go-to-guy, Austin Collie, reports "the difference between here and college is not the speed. It is the knowledge."

Knowledge is a solid predictor of success. Knowledge gained through workplace experience is six times more important than grades earned in school in predicting job performance of new employees. I contend that formal education coupled with life and job experience is a superior combination when ably applied. I have run into too many managers who have come up through the ranks exhibiting a disdain for formal education. I remember being asked to drop out of my MBA program at the University of North Carolina by a manager who professed that his MBA (mop bucket attitude) was superior. A mop bucket attitude was a way of thinking based on coming up through the ranks that imparted a high degree of familiarity with how the work was done. It was also a test of character to see if one didn't mind hard work and getting dirty. Recognizing the importance of education and having my character honed by the Marines, I declined his request and completed my degree, which opened doors previously unimagined.

The construction and restaurant industries are two industries where the path to the top has traditionally come through the ranks. This placed capable, and often successful, technical experts in senior leadership positions. But rarely were they the total package. They relied on that mop bucket attitude rather than on acquiring new knowledge. I have seen fast-food and casual dining restaurants be placed in terrible locations because leadership did not conduct solid data analysis. It was left to the gut feel of the boss who drove around the neighborhood and proclaimed it a good site. These homerun "A" locations, were soon revealed to be underperforming "C" locations to the financial distress of the entire company. A little formal knowledge in site selecction would have gone a long way in these cases.

As mentioned earlier, leaders get paid for their judgment and this is sharpened with an ever-increasing knowledge base. You can't exercise judgment if you don't have knowledge of what you are judging and the context in which you are operating. This requirement for knowledge is made more necessary in a world where information expands to fill all available time and where knowledge is increasing.

This is tough to catalog, but a look at the number of English words is a good start. The *Encyclopedia Americana* reports, "The vocabulary has grown from the 50,000 to 60,000 words in Old English to the tremendous number of entries—650,000 to 750,000—in an unabridged dictionary of today." Obviously much of the growth comes from new technology. Interestingly, about 80 percent of the words stem from Latin. You may be familiar with Moore's Law about the doubling of computer power every twenty months. This doubling enables more learning. Kurzweil analyzed history and technology and showed that technological change is exponential rather than linear. So, in his estimation, we won't experience one hundred years of progress in the twenty-first century—it will be more like 20,000 years of progress (at today's rate). Heck, the venerable *Oxford English Dictionary* will probably not survive in print in the next decade. The online *Oxford English Dictionary* now gets two million hits a month from subscribers. The current printed edition—a hefty twenty-volume, $1,165 set published in 1989—has sold about 30,000 sets in total. Need I say more?

The average person today consumes almost three times as much information as the typical person consumed in 1960, according to research at the University of California, San Diego. If you are not increasing your knowledge, you are falling behind. Peter Drucker wrote in *Post-Capitalist Society*, "Value is now created by 'productivity' and 'innovation,' both of which are applications of knowledge at work." So knowledge in the general sense is not only important, it is foundational for future success.

The Marines recognize the importance of knowledge: It is one of the traits of leadership. They define it as the understanding of a science or an art—the range of one's information, including professional knowledge and an understanding of your fellow Marines. Notice they take it from the professional to the personal. It says you must know and understand your people and what they are doing and going through.

First, this is a respect issue. Second, it is a direction issue. Employees rightly believe that if the leader doesn't know what they do and how they do it, the leader will be unable to make the right decisions on how to effectively employ them, implement changes that positively impact performance, and improve the team's ability to capitalize on future opportunities.

Let's be clear that knowledge and the pursuit of knowledge are not limited to the Fortune 500. These big firms may have huge training departments (and budgets) and regularly send employees for advanced degrees, but smaller firms can apply this principle, too. Seventy-five percent of the finalists in the 2010 Top Small Company Workplaces list offer educational assistance.

The final consideration here is the transfer of knowledge. Experience happens on the job. Learning, or knowledge, happens during the debriefing process. Post mortems, after-actions—call them what you will, the world's best organizations do a superior job in conducting these critical reviews and in communicating the learning from these reviews across the organization. The quality of the reviews is directly attributable to the interest and support of a leader who recognizes the importance of continually developing knowledge.

Successful leaders know and understand the jobs they supervise. They seek to learn about the world they operate in and are naturally curious to gain knowledge. They make sound decisions based on that knowledge, which increases their credibility and their overall effectiveness. In short, the leader of the future will be a learner who becomes more knowledgeable with time.

The good life is inspired by love and guided by knowledge.
—Bertrand Russell

KNOWLEDGE IN ACTION

American Infrastructure (AI) is a vertically integrated heavy civil contractor operating in the Mid-Atlantic states. Ranking number 166 on the ENR Top 400 list of contractors, AI was founded in 1939 and remains a highly successful contractor.

This success is based on the core values of the organization and their clear vision. The key tenets are centered on the ability to compete successfully with the best, fastest, and safest competitors in the world, to build a great place to work, and to leave footprints in our industry. This can be a challenge with over two thousand employees working across the heart of the eastern seaboard of the United States. This challenge has been met head on.

To move toward its vision, the team at AI recognized the need for more and better education for all team members. It created a continuous learning center that publishes an annual catalog of courses. The catalog looks like a course catalog you would see at the finest universities and covers technical education as well as supervisory skills. Development isn't for the chosen few; it is for the many. Ross Myers, president of AI, believes the best leaders are grown internally, and the only way to do that is to invest heavily in getting them ready to lead. Bob Capps is one of those long-time employees who has grown into a new role. He has moved from being a builder of roads to a builder of people as he has assumed positions of leadership in the education arm of AI. He explained the importance of continuous learning starting with the hourly employee up through the chain of command and went on to say, "There is a true pipeline here for developing leaders for the next level. We firmly believe this is the key to our continued success."

Training magazine has twice recognized AI on its top 125 list of firms that provide the best training in the country. It ranked third across the United States and several other countries for organizational commitment to training and for demonstrating enterprise-wide success through employee learning and development by the American Society for Training and Development. It has been recognized as one of the best places to work in Pennsylvania. Great places to work are characterized by trust, pride, and camaraderie and deliver higher financial performance. These accomplishments are noteworthy, but AI is a construction company. The true indicator of success for AI is industry recognition, of which AI has received much. Every year its projects win awards. It has stronger retention of senior employees than other construction firms. Put all this knowledge together and underpin it with solid values, and you have a profitable construction company that is among the best in the nation.

KNOWLEDGE IN ACTION (BONUS)

Co-owner of Horizon Services, Inc., Mark Aitken, says the heating, ventilating, and air conditioning (HVAC) industry has long supported employee training. He notes that some companies fear that workers who get trained could leave for another company, and their investment would be lost. "Our philosophy is, 'What if you don't train and they stay?'" The 260 employees at Horizon are required to take 100 to 150 hours of training at its headquarters in Prices Corner, Delaware. The training is necessary because HVAC systems, equipment, and procedures change, and employees have varying degrees of expertise in particular areas. For instance, some may be skilled in repairing air conditioning but not at diagnosing heat pump problems. The company ramped up its training about seven years ago after experiencing frequent customer complaints and callbacks. The company hired two full-time trainers for its offices in Delaware and Pennsylvania. "They learn how to ask questions, how to present products and services, all areas of customer service," Aitken said, adding that Horizon also provides team-building sessions and invites motivational speakers.

A TO Z APPLICATION

1. On a scale of 1–10, how do you rate on this trait? _____

2. How do you acquire new knowledge? Is this enough for you at this point in your life? _____

_____

_____

3. List someone you know who exemplifies this trait: _____

_____

4. What action *will* you do differently to improve in this area? _

_____

5. How well do you do in creating opportunities for others in
   your firm to gain knowledge? _____

_____

_____

KNOWLEDGE JUMPSTART

- Always have something to read for when you are standing in
  line or waiting for an appointment.
- Turn off the TV, the computer, and phone when you are
  reading to learn.
- Subscribe to (and read) the professional journal for your
  industry and for the industry of your major customers.
- Subscribe to and read *Executive Book Summaries*.
- Learn to listen. (Haven't we said this one already!)

LOYAL

If you live to be 100, I hope I live to be 100 minus 1 day, so I never have to live without you. —Winnie the Pooh

loy·al - Characterized by or showing faithfulness to commitments, vows, allegiance, obligations, etc. / OPPOSITE - Undependable; unfaithful

———

Loyalty is a two-way street. Today the concept of loyalty in business seems almost as naive as that of integrity—but it still matters. Perhaps it matters even more in a society where it is less prevalent. If you hope for loyalty from your people, then you must extend it to them *first.* Statesman Donald Regan said it plainly, "You've got to give loyalty down, if you want loyalty up."

The traditional, implied employment contract in the United States states that, in return for my hard work as an employee, you, as my employer, will take care of and look out for me. Workers welcome the security of this arrangement, and even though it puts companies in a somewhat "parental" role, it helps create that two-way loyalty.

On a personal level, if the boss takes the heat for the employees, they will appreciate this and work harder to prevent heat in the future. When something goes wrong, the leader says, "It was my fault," and moves on. The loyal leader doesn't throw employees in front of a bus to save his own skin. Stanford professor Robert Sutton wrote of this in a September 2010 *Harvard Business Review* article with the title "The Boss as Human Shield." In it, he quotes baseball great Ernie Banks: "I learned from Mr. Wrigley early in my career that loyalty wins and it creates friendships. I saw it work for him in his business . . . "Loyalty and friendship . . . created all the wealth I have." Cynics may say this kind of utopian workplace doesn't exist. I say that doesn't mean it isn't worth striving for.

When I was a regional manager in the restaurant business, I told my team that the customer is always right, *but* they don't have the right to treat you like dirt. And there were times when we knew the customer was *not* right, but we opted to lose the battle to win the war. There were times when the customer, right or wrong, became abusive. They became verbally and, sometimes, even physically threatening. If I was in the building at that point, I would enter the conversation and ask the customer to calm down. If they did, we could generally resolve the problem. If they refused to calm down, I would ask them again and inform them that if they could not, they would have to leave. It didn't happen often, but I am proud to say that there were times I threw people out of my restaurants—out of loyalty to my staff, of course.

Do your employees notice these things? Do they care? When it came time for me to move on from a restaurant that I had helped open, I was reminded that they do care. This restaurant was big on pins. Get certified in something, you received a pin to wear on your uniform shirt. Get a great customer comment; you got another pin. Whatever you accomplished, we had a pin for that. The pineapple has long been a symbol of hospitality in the Americas. Being hospitable means taking care of people, looking out for them—being loyal. At a going-away party for me, the team trainer made a brief speech on behalf of all the employees. Then she took a pineapple pin, one that she had earned herself, off of her lapel and gave it to me. I still have it as a reminder that loyalty matters.

This doesn't mean we don't disagree. In fact, a relationship characterized by loyalty will welcome discourse in search of the best outcome. Healthy debate behind closed doors is fine, but, once a decision is made, the group must close ranks and present a unified front. Any further action that is contrary to the good of the group or incites actions counter to the agreed-upon decision are disloyal and must be addressed by the leader.

In his book *Leadership*, former New York City Mayor Rudy Giuliani devotes an entire chapter to "Loyalty: The Vital Virtue." He gives a number of anecdotes and examples, but he takes the concept further, "It's not enough for a leader to give and receive loyalty. For loyalty to mean something, it has to be established as a culture throughout the organization." Of course, for that to have a chance of happening, the leader must set the tone.

Zell Miller, former governor of Georgia, devoted a chapter of his book to loyalty. In *Corps Values: Everything You Need to Know I Learned in the Marines*, he writes, "Of all the human instincts, the strongest and most basic is the will to survive. An essential ingredient of that will is a well-defined sense of belonging," what he calls loyalty. He describes it as the cement that binds people together. Further investigation would tell us the Marines define cohesion as putting the values of the group over the values of the individual. It implies all members of the group are loyal to the group and what it is trying to accomplish. For the layman, cohesion means sticking together. That's loyalty at its best.

As you can see, it is important for leaders to be loyal to their people. You get what you give, and if you want your employees to be loyal to you and your firm, then you need to be loyal to them first. If you treat them like an expendable number, they will act like one.

So treat them well, value their input, and let them know you care—
they will go out of their way to make you look good.

The greater the loyalty of a group toward the group, the greater is the motivation among the members to achieve the goals of the group, and the greater the probability that the group will achieve its goals. —Rensis Likert

LOYALTY IN ACTION

A division of an international heavy equipment manufacturer experienced a nearly 60 percent reduction in volume in 2009. There was simply not enough work to keep everyone in this division employed. However, there were indications that 2010 would show growth, and the manager didn't want to lose people and have to retrain new ones. He communicated with all employees to keep them fully informed. During this slow phase, they worked on solutions to cut costs and retain staff. When there was nothing left to cut, he worked with them and the state to lay off employees for 30 days at a time. He was able to preserve their health care benefits during the layoff. Legally, he was not required to do this, but he wanted to keep as many employees as possible. This layoff rotation continued for four months with about 25 percent of the workforce being idled at any one time. During this time, employee engagement scores actually increased, and when the plant returned to full production it retained 96 percent of the employees.

A TO Z APPLICATION

1. On a scale of 1–10, how do you rate on loyalty? _____

2. How do you demonstrate loyalty to your employees? _____

   _____

   _____

   _____

3. List someone you know who exemplifies this trait: _____

   _____

4. Would your employees say you are loyal to them? Have you asked them? _____

   _____

   _____

   _____

5. What actions *will* you do to improve in this area? _____

   _____

   _____

- Praise in public, criticize in private.
- Give credit and take the blame.
- Don't talk poorly about anyone on your team to anyone.
- Use "we" and "us" instead of "me" and "them" when talking about your team.
- Read *The Loyalty Effect*.

MODEL

Example is not the main thing in influencing others. It is the only thing. —Various

mod·el - A standard or example for imitation or comparison; / OPPOSITE - Pretender; fake

———

You cannot lead people from behind a desk. Stepping away from the desk allows you to accomplish several objectives: You can role-model proper behavior, inspire and influence your people, enable direct communication, and simply be visible. In Peters and Waterman's classic book *In Search of Excellence*, this technique is called "management by walking around." Despite its deceptively simple name, being a good role model is one of the most important—and sometimes difficult—elements of good leadership.

Effective leaders generally don't ask people to do something they themselves would not do. At this point in their careers, they may not actually do the thing they are asking, but they *will have* done it in the past and are capable of doing it now.

Early in the morning on the day I got commissioned as a second lieutenant of the Marines, our group went on a three-mile run. Joining us was the dad of one of the graduates, a Marine colonel. So here was this "old guy" running with us. As we finished the run around the lake at the University of Notre Dame, we went amphibious and all ran into the lake and started swimming across. The colonel was right there—step by step, stroke by stroke. Years later I served in his unit, and I knew first-hand that he would never ask us to do something he would not do himself. Compare that to another colonel I worked for who refused to fly the dangerous night missions and scheduled as few as possible for our unit, leaving us poorly prepared for combat situations. He was a weak role model; we couldn't wait to get out of that unit.

Dwight D. Eisenhower had a keen understanding of leadership. After the invasion of North Africa in 1942, he said, "Optimism and pessimism are infectious and they spread more rapidly from the head downward than in any other direction. Optimism has a most extraordinary effect upon all with whom the commander comes in contact. With this clear realization, I firmly determined that my mannerisms and speech in public would always reflect the cheer-ful certainty of victory—that any pessimism and discouragement I might ever feel would be reserved for my pillow."

Psychologists confirm what Eisenhower knew and have observed that bad habits can spread through an office like a contagious disease. Employees tend to mirror the bad behaviors of their coworkers, with factors as diverse as low morale, poor working habits, and theft from employer all rising based on the negative behavior of peers. People are looking for role models. There is even a website, *rolemodel.net*, on this very subject. Website notwithstanding, your employees will look to you—the boss—and model your habits. You are always leading by example, whether you intend to or not. What remains is for you to model the proper behavior with a positive example.

The old saying, "A good example has twice the value of good advice" makes my point. Consider the "Do as I say, not as I do" supervisor. We've probably all worked for this individual at one time or another. We don't trust or respect him, but we do adopt his bad habits. Does he pick up a stray piece of trash from the floor, delegate that task, or worse, ignore it? If the boss stops to pick up garbage, everyone gets the message that if the leader can do it, we all can do it.

What about safety? If it isn't important to the boss, it will not be important to the employees. Leaders should model proper customer service, safety, communication, punctuality, listening, and so much more. In fact, a piece of advice given to aspiring leaders is to *watch the boss*. CareerBuilder.com listed observing leadership qualities of the boss and then emulating them as one of the top ways to accelerate your move into a leadership position.

I was collaborating with the Disney Institute (the business consulting/education arm of Disney Corporation) on a project and was given a behind-the-scenes tour of Walt Disney World. I learned about the specific spacing of garbage cans on Main Street, USA, and that, among all the 65,000 employees in Disney World Orlando, none was given the title of custodian or janitor. It was up to *all* the employees to keep the park clean (with the help of visitors who will walk only so far to put something in a trash can). What made an insightful demonstration even more interesting was the consultants picking up trash as we walked through the park. We did not walk by a single piece.

Saint Francis of Assisi instructed, "Preach the Gospel and, when necessary, use words." His point was that you can talk to people all day long and not convince them, but *show them* and they might believe you. The Marines take appearance pretty seriously. It's part of that whole "attention to detail" thing. They cite bearing as one of their leadership traits and define it as "creating a favorable impression in carriage, appearance, and personal conduct at all times." Quite simply, as a Marine officer, I had to adhere to an ideal in my conduct and appearance. How could I take a Marine to task for being out-of-uniform—wearing the wrong color socks with his boots, for example—if I was out-of-uniform in some way, too? Clearly, I couldn't. In physical training, I wasn't the fastest, but I certainly worked the hardest and sent the message that that was what I expected.

I was no choirboy when I joined the Marines, but there is no doubt that my use of profanity was refined in that setting. This is one of my biggest failings today. As a parent, I cringe whenever I use such vocabulary with my kids around, and I know it is as much a habit as anything. I have been working on it, but when I hear them using the words I used, I am reminded that I am a role model 24/7/365, and I can be a good one . . . or not.

Setting the example is not conditional; it is an *all the time* requirement. It isn't a new concept, either. Samurai Hojo Soun wrote in the 1500s, "Get up early in the morning to set a good example for your servants and to carry out your own duties as well. If you begin to be lax, you will be fired."

In the twenty-first century, the way we apply the principle may differ, but the principle itself is constant. When the stakes are high and the risks great, this is even more vital. Leaders set the example through physical courage and, more important, through moral courage. They always do the right thing. Demonstrate the right thing, and be a model for your people to follow.

What you are doing is screaming so loudly, I can't hear you. —*Unknown*

MODEL IN ACTION

Louis Gabanna is the chairman of COLAS North America. COLAS NA is a multibillion-dollar road builder with operations in the United States and Canada. If employees have any doubt as to how they are to conduct themselves, they need look no further than their chairman. There are any number of things that set him apart. He is a fierce combination of drive for results with a clear understanding of the importance of motivating and taking care of people. He makes commitments and delivers on them. He is a gentleman.

Every year COLAS University conducts a number of programs that require managers to come to a central location for a week to nine days. Louis works with his vice president of human resources to schedule these programs eleven months ahead of time. This ensures he has these dates on his calendar so he can be available to address classes at closing graduations. Everything else that gets on his calendar subsequent to the education programs must fit around the programs. He is committed to attending and he does. In ten years he has only missed one closing, and it was due to a death in his family.

When he addresses the classes, he consistently talks about corporate values with a focus on integrity, career development, and corporate strategy. After his comments, he opens the floor for questions from the class. In doing so, he models the openness in communication that he feels is so important for his organization to succeed. Although he sets a fine example, he is concerned about how his employees carry themselves and interact with customers, suppliers, and the public. This concern has heightened with the influx of Gen Xers into management and Gen Ys into the company. He decided to institute etiquette training for his new managers.

In matters of personal recognition, the routine gift will not suffice. He is very focused on recognizing people with gifts and incentives that matter to the recipient. Play golf with him and you will not only get COLAS logo golf balls, you may also get a COLAS golf towel with your name embroidered on it. This personal touch extends far beyond golf towels, but it is always there.

Maintaining his composure at all times, he is unflappable. While he is quick to enjoy a laugh, he restrains himself from showing disappointment with employees. He expects them to have the details on an issue and be ready to discuss them. Just as he models full disclosure and openness, he expects it in return. He knows this is the best chance he has to get unfiltered information with which to make sound decisions.

Gabanna has risen to the very top of one of the most successful construction companies in the world by working hard, producing results, and creating a great team. He serves as a role model for people inside of and outside of the organization and is respected by all.

A TO Z APPLICATION

1. On a scale of 1–10, how do you rate on this trait? _____

2. What about your behavior do you wish were different? _____

_____

_____

_____

3. Who is a role model for you? _____

_____

4. For whom are you a role model? _____

_____

_____

5. What action *will* you do to improve in this area?_____

_____

_____

_____

MODEL JUMPSTART

- Look in a mirror; are you pleased with what you see?
- Control your language.
- Describe expected behavior, then live it.
- Read *Leadership Presence.*
- Smile (another one we have seen before!).

NOBLE

A noble person attracts noble people, and knows how to hold on to them.
—*Johann Wolfgang von Goethe*

no·ble - Of an exalted moral or mental character or excellence; lofty; admirable in dignity of conception, manner of expression, execution / OPPOSITE - Unimpressive; base; mean; ignoble; vulgar

———

You would not typically think of nobility as a characteristic of leadership. I say this because I firmly believe that leadership is not a title or birthright; it is action and relationship. But the definition of noble embodies exalted character and admirable expression and execution. Sounds like what we need in a good leader.

When most people think of nobility, they think of a class of people distinguished by their birthright or rank. They are the "blue bloods." In Europe they would be the dukes and duchesses, earls and countesses, and barons and baronesses. Some of these people have led with great distinction. They have led nobly. Some have not. An unattributed quote emphasizes this point, "I have seen soldiers panic at the first sight of battle and a wounded squire pulling arrows out from his wound to fight and save his dying horse. Nobility is not a birthright but is defined by one's action."

What actions then should we look for to define nobility? What does it really mean to be noble? And can nobility be a leadership trait? Absolutely! Perhaps it is as simple as the distinction between class and crass. I don't think anybody would dispute that legendary UCLA basketball coach John Wooden was a class act. He lived by the motto, "You can't live a perfect day without doing something for someone who will never be able to repay you." He made everyone around him a better person and instilled in them a desire to excel. American poet James Russell Lowell could have been writing about Wooden (although he was writing a century earlier) "Be noble! And the nobleness that lies in other men, sleeping, but never dead, will rise in majesty to meet thine own."

The noble leader does not disparage others and doesn't take the cheap shot. In our sound bite society where the sharp reply gets the headlines, it is difficult to picture the better leader being the one to hold his tongue. Sarcasm and putdowns may work in comedy clubs and locker rooms, but they don't work in the workplace. This would extend to profanity. I confess I am not an exemplar in this, but I hope to live up to the expectation of my father who asked me once when he heard me drop a few choice words, "Do you talk like that in front of your girlfriend? Why would you do that? You have an education and are better than that." Ouch. Still working on it, Pop.

James V. O'Connor, author of *Cuss Control*, writes "the problem with foul language is we use it too often, failing to communicate clearly, ignoring sensitivities of others, and damaging the perception we want people to have of us." Foul language isn't the worst thing you can do, but you can do better. Mark Twain noted "in certain trying circumstances, urgent circumstances, desperate circumstances, profanity furnishes a relief denied even in prayer." To curse is human; to curse a lot is to be ignoble. At the end of the day, it is just plain lazy.

Riccardo Muti is an Italian conductor that served as the tenth music director of the Chicago Symphony Orchestra. There are books and classes on what we can learn about leadership from an orchestra. Muti writes, "Nobility of spirit has more to do with simplicity than ostentation, wisdom rather than wealth, commitment rather than ambition."

But how do you know if you have the nobility we are discussing? Give yourself the "five friends test." Take a look around at who you would consider your five best friends. Although each one is unique, as a group they will share certain traits and characteristics. Their traits are your traits. If you don't like what you see, you may need to find some new friends.

There is nothing noble in being superior to your fellow men. True nobility lies in being superior to your former self. —Elijah Wood

NOBILITY IN ACTION

Robert A. Kinsley is the founder of Kinsley Construction. It can be difficult to characterize men like him, but the phrase "he is a great American" is a good start. His rise to prominence is a direct result of his hard work and his respect for people. At 5' 7" he cuts a wide swath with his passion and presence—he is a noble giant.

Founded in 1963, his company began as a subcontracting firm in the concrete trade. Two years later, site excavation, paving, and utility installation services were added. In the 1970s the company entered the general contracting market, yet retained its own tradespeople. Steel erection was added to the list of services, and its success led to the addition of Kinsley Manufacturing, which has become one of the largest and most efficient steel fabricators in the mid-Atlantic region. Kinsley ranked at number 136 on the 2010 ENR list of the Top 400 general contractors.

Even with five highly competent sons running much of the business today, who are now responsible for all of the family business and extensive real estate holdings, Bob remains an active chairman and continues to exercise influence in the firm and in the community. From a humble beginning, Bob has risen to a place of prominence in the community. Although he is a builder, he is also a conserver. He recognizes the importance of economic growth for his community while understanding the importance of conservation and preservation. He's a founding member of the Farm and Natural Lands Trust of York County. He and his family have placed perpetual conservation easements on nearly 1,800 acres of the family farm in Southern Pennsylvania and on over 700 acres in Northern Maryland.

Once, when touring a large jobsite, he noticed 2600 evergreens that would have to be cleared for a utility right of way. At that moment he hatched the idea of giving every employee a potted Christmas tree for the holiday.

While he will always be known for Kinsley Construction, perhaps his greatest legacy, beyond his family, is in the new museum at the Gettysburg National Military Park. Recognizing the need for a modern, yet reverent, tribute to that turning point in our history, Bob and his wife Anne acquired land and proposed a new facility. Through countless hours, dollars, and struggles, the museum is a shining new reality. While it may have eventually been built without Bob, the fact that Bob was involved ensured it got built. He was involved in every phase of the project from concept to funding, design, and dedication. He understands that Gettysburg was more than a battle. Historians have come to believe that this was the most defining moment in the history of our nation. It impacted lives across our nation, and he wants those stories to be remembered. As a self-performing general contractor, Bob is always thinking about the people who do the actual work.

There aren't many people who build great construction companies while giving Christmas trees as employee gifts while helping our nation get a new museum. There are some noble people who do.

A TO Z APPLICATION

1. On a scale of 1–10, how do you rate on nobility? _____

2. Are you more class or crass? _____

   _____

3. List someone you know who exemplifies this trait: _____

   _____

   _____

4. List your five friends and five traits you admire: _____

_____

_____

_____

_____

5. What action *will* you do to improve in this area?_____

_____

_____

NOBILITY JUMPSTART

- Dress the part and speak the part.
- Learn to shake hands and make meaningful eye contact.
- Take the five friends test.
- What is your higher purpose?
- Read *Lions Don't Need to Roar.*

OPEN MINDED

There exist limitless opportunities in every industry. Where there is an open mind, there will always be a frontier. —*Charles F. Kettering*

o·pen mind·ed - Having or showing a mind receptive to new ideas or arguments; unprejudiced; unbigoted; impartial / OPPOSITE - Closed minded; small minded

———

Leaders need information to make decisions. If you don't have an open mind, you can't get all the information you need to make decisions. Sometimes leaders think they already have all the answers. Years of experience and expertise will do that to you. In fact, senior leaders are often the least open to new ideas, which makes them the most likely to miss opportunities.

In my book *No Yelling*, I talk about how developing excellent technical proficiency can actually lead to trouble. People who have been doing something for a long time generally develop expertise in that area. We expect this, and it is a good thing. Problems arise when this expertise rules out any other option. Lack of an open mind can cost money. Research on financial managers found that 95 percent display a particular commitment to sectors in which they experienced their first success. Ultimately, this tendency leads to missed buying opportunities in other segments of the market, as well as unrealistic enthusiasm for their chosen sector. An open mind leaves a chance for someone to drop a worthwhile thought into it.

Jane Goodall, considered by some to be the world's foremost authority on chimpanzees, was not trained as a scientist. When she went into the bush to simply observe the chimps, she was criticized for her methods. But in doing this, she gained a world of knowledge. Her advice to new scientists: Forget what you learned and just be with the animals. She tells students, "One of the most important things—sometimes the hardest thing—is to have an open mind." Basketball coach Phil Jackson took it one step further, advising his players to "Always keep an open mind and a compassionate heart." Noted expert on human behavior, Abraham Maslow, observed, "The novice can often see things the expert overlooks."

Other reasons to be open minded are to foster creativity in your people and to demonstrate respect. If you don't *give* respect, you certainly won't *get* it. Employees want to be heard; they want to know that their opinions matter. Being open minded is about being receptive to new ideas and new information. There is nothing more demotivating to an employee than to come up with an idea and eagerly bring it to the boss only to have it discarded with little thought and even less recognition.

If leadership is about change for better results, then being receptive can only help. The pace of change is rapid, and it is impossible for any one person to have a grip on all that is going on. In the good ol' days (last century), it was possible. Not today. Having an open mind means knowing you need a little help with it all. In his book *Never Wrestle with a Pig*, famed sports agent Mark McCormack speaks of "locked-room logic." He found that putting people together in a room to solve a problem will probably *not* solve the problem. In fact, it will likely yield more of the same thinking that led to the problem in the first place. He explains, "You have to open the door and let some fresh faces in. The people who will have the biggest impact on your business are probably not in it right now."

Read that again: *The people who will have the biggest impact on your business are probably not in it right now.* Wow. Who do you need to be talking to that you are not?

Having an open mind means embracing people who are different—and letting it pay off for you. Workplace teams composed of different personality types are 14 percent more productive than teams composed of more "like" individuals. I once worked with a consultant who had a style that was 180 degrees opposite to my own. As a result, he was very annoying to work with. However, we produced great results, and I learned to respect him and ask for his input because I knew it would be solid.

You can cultivate an open mind. Listen to different music, look at art, or write backwards. Try a new food, learn to juggle, or write a letter to the editor. Ride a roller coaster, maybe do some traveling or a jigsaw puzzle—any number of things that may be slightly out of the norm for you. Be quiet and listen to your people and consider the merits of their point of view. Just be . . . *open*.

Above all, remember that the most important thing you can take anywhere is not a Gucci bag or French-cut jeans; it's an open mind. —*Gail Rubin Bereny*

OPEN MINDED IN ACTION

After conducting a program for construction superintendents and foremen on communication skills, I was approached by a burly veteran. With a gray mustache and leathered skin from too much time outside on projects, he said, "I gotta tell ya. I have been coming to training like this for a bunch of years now." He paused, and I braced myself for the predicted comment about it being a waste of time and how employees don't work hard anymore. I listened as he said, "I am fifty-three years old, and I have been in construction for thirty-five years. I came to this company three years ago, at age fifty, to be closer to my grandkids. When I came, I recognized I had a chance to do things differently. All the things you talked about. The leadership, the communication, and the motivation . . . I made a commitment to start doing that when I got here. And I gotta tell ya, the past three years have been the best three years I have ever had in construction."

He got my attention, and I asked him to tell me more. He then gave specific examples from his old company about how he had handled situations. These all had less than ideal outcomes. He then related similar situations from his new company and his new approach. Unlike the stories from his previous experiences, these had generally favorable endings. He also admitted it took some effort to change old habits but affirmed that where there is a will there is a way, and for him it started with having an open mind.

A TO Z APPLICATION

1. On a scale of 1–10, how do you rate on being open minded?_

   _____

2. When is the last time you changed your opinion on something? _____

_____

_____

3. List someone you know who exemplifies this trait: _____

_____

4. In what areas are you most likely to reject new ideas? Why? _

_____

_____

5. What action *will* you do to improve in this area?_____

_____

_____

OPEN-MINDED JUMPSTART

- Read something different.
- Take an improvization class.
- Do something different.
- Drive home using a different route.
- Look for points of agreement—not disagreement. Listen more.

POWER

Lions don't need to roar. —*Debra Benton*

pow·er - Ability to do or act; having the capability of doing or accomplishing something / OPPOSITE - Weak; impotent; lacking impact or authority

———

"Because I said so." If you are a parent, you have uttered these words. If you have had a parent, you have heard them. These words represent brute power at its worst. There is no reason offered, no mitigating graciousness. It is force, pure and simple. My experience has taught me that this doesn't really work in parenting, and my experience as a leader has taught me that it definitely doesn't work in the supervisor/employee relationship.

We often use power and control to get things done and sometimes to justify our authority. But it's important to remember that, while we can really only control a few people, we can influence many.

Our ultimate source of power does not come from the authority vested in us by the "Powers That Be." It comes from *your people* who buy into what you are trying to accomplish and are willing to run through walls to help you do it.

History reminds us that power is not always a good attribute. We often have an inherent distrust of authority figures. Centuries ago, those in power could have you put to death, simply because they could. Today, those in power seem to play by a different set of rules than the rest of us, again because they can. As former President Bill Clinton so notoriously told newsman Dan Rather in a TV interview, I cheated "because I could."

But power need not be a scary concept. In fact, we use it every day. Power moves us from potential to action. When used correctly, power and leadership can be intimate allies. Jeffrey Pfeffer, professor of organizational behavior at Stanford University, is the author of *Power: Why Some People Have It—And Others Don't*, and power is the focus of his teaching. One of his primary lesson points is that you "must make peace with power." In other words, it is not an inherently bad thing. He also maintains you will not get far if you are unable to build and use power.

Al Gini, co-founder and editor of *Business Ethics Quarterly*, writes, "To have power is to possess the capacity to control or direct change. All forms of leadership must make use of power. The central issue of power in leadership is not 'will it be used?' But rather 'will it be used wisely and well?'"

Well said. A person has the potential for influencing five bases of power over another. Researchers John French and Bertram Raven identify these:

1. Coercive Power—Effectiveness based on fear. A person with coercive power can make things difficult for people. These are the people you want to avoid getting angry. Employees working under coercive managers are unlikely to be committed and more likely to resist the manager. This is the "because I said so" boss noted earlier.

2. Reward Power—Compliance is achieved based on the ability to distribute rewards that others view as valuable. You might find it advantageous to trade favors with him or her.

3. Legitimate Power—Authority a person holds due to his or her position in the formal hierarchy of an organization. This person has the right, considering his or her position and your job responsibilities, to expect you to comply with valid requests.

4. Expert Power—Influence based on special skills or knowledge. This person earns respect because of accumulated experience, education, and/or insight. Expert power is most strongly and consistently related to effective employee performance.

5. Referent Power—Influence based on possession of desirable resources or personal traits. This supervisor may have been given his or her authority because of good looks or a gregarious personality rather than any aptitude for the job. But people may enjoy working for them for those reasons.

So power essentially comes from one of two places: the position (reward, legitimate, expert) or the person (coercive, referent, expert). Both are important. But what we must recognize is that power really comes from action. It is what I actually do that really matters and adds to or decreases my power. In reality, a leader obtains the best results by skillfully combining positional power and influential power in his life.

As the saying goes, "You can catch more flies with honey than with vinegar." In other words, persuade me, educate me, influence me. Don't bully me. And I will gladly work even harder for you.

Power consists of one's capacity to link his will with the purpose of others, to lead by reason and a gift of cooperation. —Woodrow Wilson

POWER IN ACTION

Ask Barry Schlouch, founder and principle of Schlouch Incorporated, how he turned an initial $2000 capital investment into an ENR Top 600 specialty contractor, and he will tell you one step at a time. In nearly thirty years he has moved his business from humble beginnings in the basement of his house to being one of the best places to work in Pennsylvania. His initial formula for success is simple: mastery of the trade (competency), integrity, and hard work. He firmly believes that regularly taking positive action on these critical elements is the foundation on which all else follows. In fact, he started our interview saying, "True power comes from taking action." He works tirelessly to help others learn the same lesson. Done well, these three elements give you credibility that causes people to listen to you. When people are listening you have influence, and when you have influence you have power. Consider some of these actions.

A comprehensive training program, "Roadmap to Excellence," gives employees the skills and confidence they need to perform at the highest level. Barry states, "Our focus is on the personal growth of our team to support our company's high standards." He conducts a biweekly coaching conference call for all employees. In late 2009 Schlouch recognized the challenges his clients were facing with the slowdown in the economy. He asked his employees two questions: What can I do to help you, and what can we do to help our clients? This supportive, yet challenging, dialogue is common for Barry. His employees responded with their characteristic candor and innovation. They validated processes and worked to better understand client needs to ensure they were delivering maximum value to the client. The payoff for this inquiry and effort? In summer 2010, customer satisfaction reached an all-time high.

While the principles of success are timeless, he does admit his definition of mastery has evolved over time. From the initial concept of mastery of trade, he now looks at mastery in four areas: health, family, career, and philanthropy. In each area he sets goals and works toward them. These actions enable him to repeat the growth and credibility process.

In mastery of career, Barry knew he needed more than that C average he got in high school. Learning and development is an important element of his success. He is a certified equipment manager (CEM). For eleven years he participated in the Harvard University executive education program for members of the Young Presidents Association (YPO) while also completing a two-year executive leadership program at the Wharton Business School. With all that, Barry will still be the first to tell you that all that education means nothing unless you apply it.

On a recent Thursday he spoke to fifteen emerging entrepreneurs in their 20s. During the session he asked if they wanted to live a life of greatness. Of course, all answered yes. He then asked about their goals list and how it supported that life of greatness, and most were able to report they had goals in place. His final question was what actions they were taking in the next seven days to move them toward their goals. The room was silent. They were missing the critical element of taking action. He challenged them to write down some tangible actions and invited them to send him an e-mail by midnight on Friday. They all nodded and said they would write. Only two of them did. On Thursday night he sent each of them a hand-written note expressing his confidence in them and challenging them to find and harness their true power that comes from within.

Schlouch doesn't seek power, but he has learned how to create it and leverage it for the greater good. At its core, I would assert that is what leadership is all about.

A TO Z APPLICATION

1. On a scale of 1–10, how do you rate on the effective understanding and use of power?_____

2. Your use of power:

ABLE TO USE THIS	ACTUALLY USE THIS
Coercive	Coercive
Reward	Reward
Legitimate	Legitimate
Expert	Expert
Referent	Referent

3. List someone you know who exemplifies the use of this trait:

_____

4. What specific things can you do to improve in this area? _____

_____

_____

_____

5. What action *will* you take to improve in this area? _____

_____

_____

POWER JUMPSTART

- Explain, don't demand.
- Look at an organization chart for your group. Who has the power? Why?
- Be diligent about using rewards and punishment.
- Cultivate allies/win enemies over.
- Read *Power: Why Some People Have It—and Others Don't.*

QUALITY

It is easier to do a job right than to explain why you didn't. —*Martin Van Buren*

qual·i·ty - High grade; superiority; excellence / OPPOSITE - Substandard; cheap; shoddy

———

My father had a couple of pet sayings. One of his favorites was, "If you had time to do it right the second time . . . you had time to do it right the first time." Man, that was hard to take—because I knew he was right. His other line was, "Did you do your best?" The issue of quality has gotten a lot of attention lately. *Six Sigma*, *TQM*, and *Lean* have all helped to improve quality around the globe. W Edwards Deming may have said, "Quality is everyone's responsibility," but it is the leader who establishes and communicates the standard of quality desired.

Fifty years ago the words *Made in Japan* meant an item was of poor quality. But the Japanese made a serious effort to improve their workmanship, and gradually they (and other countries) eclipsed the United States in quality manufacturing. Not only could they do it better, but they could do it at lower cost and often more quickly. The Holy Grail of faster-better-cheaper had been found. What we now know is that this level of quality is elusive; as you reach one level, you aim for the next. Such is the nature of continuous improvement in business. Margins are tight and will remain that way. When you look at the profit and loss statement for any business, there isn't a line for rework. Quality is the key. It is the ante in the game of business. High quality has multiple payoffs. It means less waste, less rework, fewer rejections, fewer complaints, and fewer returns. All this leads to lower costs and higher productivity.

The Deming Chain Reaction, named after quality guru W. Edwards Deming, illustrates this: Ultimately, increased productivity leads to increased market share, and that leads to job security— truly a win-win outcome.

This enables a firm to stay in business and provide more jobs. But before all this can happen, quality must start in the mind of the leader. Author Bob Moawad puts it this way: "Quality begins on the inside, and then works its way out." Deming goes on to say that quality is *everyone's* business. I say that no one will make it their business if the leader doesn't set the standard, talk the talk, and walk the walk on quality.

Here's an interesting note about managers thinking and acting on quality: Managers of production facilities who are meeting their quality targets actually invest *20 percent more time* in improving their practices than managers who are falling short of their goals. So those delivering better quality *work harder* to deliver *even better* quality. Welcome to corporate competition in the twenty-first century.

I recently interviewed customers of one of my road-building clients. I wanted to know their definition of great service. Every one of them replied, "Quality." Of course, this end result of "quality" comes from the diligent efforts of many people in the value chain, but it starts with a leader who sets the standard. William A. Foster put it this way, "Quality is never an accident; it is always the result of high intention, sincere effort, intelligent direction, and skillful execution. It represents the wise choice of many alternatives."

Quality breeds quality. Aristotle told us that excellence is a habit. Speaker, author, and teacher Don Miguel Ruiz writes in *The Four Agreements*, "If you do your best always, over and over again, you will become a master of transformation. Practice makes the master. By doing your best, you become a master." By doing your best, you will make Dad proud, too—and set yourself up for more quality experiences to come.

We all have higher expectations today than we did a generation—or even a decade—ago. It is important to recognize the distinction between *product quality* and *service quality*. Data confirms that many products are of higher quality today. It also confirms that the quality of services we receive is declining. This downslide confirms the need for leaders to maintain pressure in this area. Do you ever really know what kind of service to expect when you go to McDonald's, the airport, or just about anywhere else these days? We accept poor service, telling ourselves that "you get what you pay for," or "it could have been worse," or "that's just how it is these days." Witness the explosion of customer-activated kiosks (from ATMs to self check-in and self check-out). Service is so bad we would rather handle it ourselves than put up with poor quality often caused by poor leadership. Leaders must be clear about quality and why it matters. Mediocrity will not suffice today. It may be easy, but it certainly is not lasting.

One of the rarest things that a man ever does is do the best he can. —*Josh Billings*

QUALITY IN ACTION

Bill is an experienced superintendent on large commercial and institutional flooring jobs in New York City. Once in a while to catch his breath he will take some work closer to his home in Pennsylvania. He does piecework on these jobs and doesn't supervise the jobs. He works on his hands and knees side-by-side with the young guns. On a daily basis he does not install as much as these other men. When he first started working for this company, the owner recognized Bill was using more adhesive than had been estimated. While the other guys were right on target for production and adhesive usage, Bill was slightly slower and using more adhesive.

Bill politely listened to the owner when confronted and replied that in this instance more adhesive was called for, and in the long run it would be cheaper than having to redo the floor if not enough adhesive was used. The owner berated Bill for not following his plan and for his lack of knowledge. Bill smiled and went back to work. The job ended, and Bill returned to New York City.

A few months later he was again on a job for the Pennsylvania company, and the same adhesive issue returned. When confronted about high usage, Bill asked the owner how the previous job had gone. He specifically asked if there were any problems with the tile he installed, to which the owner replied no. He then asked if the other installers had any problems, to which the owner had to reply yes. Much of the tile they installed didn't stay down. In their haste to make more money and use less adhesive, the quality of their work was poor. The company had to go back and redo the rooms the other installers had done. Of course this rework was paid for by the owner at his own expense. Nothing had to be done to the rooms that Bill had done.

QUALITY IN ACTION (BONUS)

Jacobs Engineering had the contract for project management of a $150 million medium security prison in the central valley of California. We had a team of twenty-two onsite construction managers and engineers, many with years of experience building large complex projects.

The senior project manager, Chris Meyer, insisted on "inspect what you expect." He required us to be where quality was happening—to go out and see the job from a quality perspective and an end user viewpoint. "Leading quality" was another cryptic term he used. At first I didn't understand the expressions and resented having to break away from the daily "routine" of building to get out and walk the job.

Chris insisted we memorize quantities and specifications—how many square feet of this, how many cubic yards of that, and on and on until we could recite the vital statistics of the various buildings by heart. The most complicated components were the electrical and security systems. We spent four full days in a conference room with the plans and specifications scattered on tables and taped to the walls, tracing the circuits of every electrical and security system. We knew every part, piece, where it was connected, and to what. It was pizza every day until we proved we understood everything. This focus on doing it right paid off.

Almost perfection! No unresolved change orders, no claims, on time, on schedule, and we outpaced another (same footprint) identical prison forty miles away that started six months after us. They worked sixty hours a week, and we worked thirty-five to forty hours in a relaxed environment. The other project got the benefit of having us identify all the design errors, and still we finished way ahead of them. All of these results were achieved because we focused on the quality of the process, the quality of installation, and on professionally delivering a quality job.

A TO Z APPLICATION

1. On a scale of 1–10, how do you rate on quality? _____

2. What is your definition of quality? _____

_____

_____

3. List someone you know who exemplifies this trait: _____

_____

_____

4. How do your customers describe your quality? How do you know? _____

_____

_____

_____

5. What action *will* you do to improve in this area?_____

_____

_____

_____

QUALITY JUMPSTART

- Measure/track/record/display critical success factors.
- Raise your standards. What was good enough yesterday isn't good enough today.
- Communicate the new standards.
- Read anything by Deming.
- Facilitate a discussion at work to define quality for your team.

RESULTS ORIENTED

Git 'er done! —*Larry the Cable Guy*

re·sult - A desirable or beneficial consequence, outcome, or effect / OPPOSITE - Unproductive; unfocused

——

The world is full of people who talk a good game. They make plans, promises, and excuses. But they rarely produce results. In sports there are winners and losers. The difference is clear: The winners get the job done. They produce results in the form of points. There are gracious winners and sometimes there are ugly winners. As hockey great Bobby Orr put it, "Forget about style; worry about results." Leaders would do well to heed his advice.

You know that saying, "The road to hell is paved with good intentions"? Well, the earliest version of that phrase has been attributed to Saint Bernard of Clairvaux (1091–1153) as, "Hell is full of good intentions or desires." Scholars don't quite know when the road was added, but we get the point. Just because you want something to happen doesn't mean it will happen. Yes, thought precedes action that, in turn, precedes results. But *directed* action is still required. Or, as General Gordon R. Sullivan, US Army (Ret) liked to say, "Hope is not a method." I can hope to lose weight. Or I can change my eating habits, exercise more, and actually lose weight.

Speaking of losing weight, Camilio Cruz, PhD is the author of *Once Upon a Cow*. A recent survey on his website showed that 90 percent of people chose not having enough time as the primary reason (excuse?), or as Cruz would say, *cow*, to justify not working out. Let me explain: In poor societies, owning a cow is often viewed as a blessing. In fact, despite living in abject poverty, a family is considered wealthy if they own a cow. The cow then becomes an excuse for not moving forward, perhaps out of poverty. Cruz writes that the metaphor of the cow is about getting rid of bad habits, excuses, limiting attitudes, and false beliefs that keep people bound to mediocrity. I would add that getting rid of the cow is about finally producing results. The poor economy in 2009–2010 was a huge cow for many businesses—but not all. Some kept investing and doing what they could to improve their results at that time and to deliver even better results when the economy eventually recovered.

Terry Orlick, in *Embracing Your Potential*, writes that life satisfaction is 22 percent more likely for those with a steady stream
of minor accomplishments for than those who express interest in
achieving only major accomplishments. For Americans who love
the home run, this may be bad news. When we talk of productivity improvement in the United States, we disdain the incremen-
tal *kaizen* approach. But maybe the lean practitioners are on to
something. Results matter, and it appears a stream of results matters more for your own satisfaction and the ultimate success of the
team. In youth baseball, players are sometimes told, "A walk is as
good as a hit." And four walks equals one home run. In both cases,
a point is scored.

Larry Bossidy, former CEO of Allied Signal, talks about results
in his book *Execution*. At face value, execution is about getting
things done; it is about results. However, Bossidy goes further to
explain that it is the *execution* that enables you to deliver results;
results don't simply happen by themselves. Execution is a systematic
way of exposing reality and acting on it. The problem is that many
firms don't accept reality very well. Therefore, they don't execute and
don't deliver results. Winston Churchill recognized this when he
said, "However beautiful the strategy, you should occasionally look
at the results." Bossidy goes on, "The leader must be in charge of
getting things done by running three core processes—picking other

leaders, setting the strategic direction, and conducting operations." Clearly, a results orientation is just the start. *Delivering* results is where leaders truly gain credibility.

Leaders also help others deliver results. Holding people accountable for results is part of their work. Ideally, employees are self-motivated to deliver results, but sometimes they do need to be managed. When I was a regional manager for Arby's Restaurants, one of the key costs we looked at was food cost. Labor was important. Every month I ranked my managers by various lines on their P&L. Those with the best scores were recognized and rewarded. For worst food cost I had an award, too—a rubber chicken. We handed it out with great ceremony, and the recipient was required to hang it in their office. It was a tongue-in-cheek way to underscore a very important issue. No manager ever won the rubber chicken award two months in a row.

There are plenty of smart people out there who don't accomplish anything. Early twentieth-century Lebanese-American poet Kahlil Gibran, author of *The Prophet*, stated, "A little knowledge that acts is worth infinitely more than much knowledge that is idle." McDonald's founder Ray Kroc said, "The world is full of talented failures, people who lack nothing in the way of education, ability, and charm, but never seem to make it. The missing ingredient, the difference between success and failure is determination, the will to press on." They had everything they needed, but they produced no results.

Contrast these people with Rowan. Who? Rowan is the fellow called upon by President William McKinley in *A Message to Garcia* to hand-deliver a message to the rebel Cuban leader, Garcia. Rowan accepted the mission and began his journey to Cuba to find Garcia. He didn't ask any questions of the president; he just got going and delivered the letter. Throughout the journey, Rowan was focused on the desired result. You can read his account of the mission online in *How I Carried the Message to Garcia*.

I often remind myself and others not to confuse effort with results. A Google search indicates a lot of other folks say it, too. However, how many actually *do* it? Results make me high. They give me a positive feeling that carries over into other areas of my life. I feel good when I work out. I feel good when I return phone calls promptly. I feel good when I get my desk or the garage cleaned. I feel good when I do a great job for a client. As I wrote this book, I felt good. Results create a wave of success for you to ride to higher, greater successes. Results also instill trust and confidence in you from others. If leaders are to influence, they must be trusted. Delivering on what you say you will do is the fast lane to trust.

Effective leadership is not about making speeches or being liked; leadership is defined by results, not attributes. —Peter Drucker

RESULTS ORIENTATION IN ACTION

At the time it was going to be the one of the longest runways in the United States. Changes to mix designs by the owner for the asphalt shoulders caused delays and disruptions to the schedule. The delays pushed the job into the winter months in Colorado. The contract required that work be suspended during the winter. However, this delay created the potential for liquidated damages. With this backdrop Jeff Wankea, vice president of operations for Sturgeon Electric, explained what came next.

> We had to make a decision. We could take our chances in court, or we could take a different approach on the job. We could work during the winter or shut the job down and take our chances in the spring with the thaw and mud. We decided to work. The owner and the FAA allowed the winter work to proceed as long as Sturgeon Electric paid for all of the associated costs (e.g., inspectors' overtime, security, and utilities). Like the Inchon landing in the Korean War, where few gave it a chance of success, the winter work proved to be the turning point. It changed the outcome of the entire project and made it a victory for everyone involved in the project.

We *calculated* the potential effects of working in winter weather, we worked with the union for compensation if we got snowed out, we calculated the effect of the spring melt and accumulated water and mud. We found out how many days of sun we could expect in Colorado that time of year. Every four hours we measured production for very specific items, e.g. feet of cable pulled and number of connections by crew. We posted the results in a very conspicuous place. Everyone knew it was "be productive or go home." The scoreboard doesn't lie.

With everyone on board, we focused on hourly, daily, and weekly results. Everyone knew the score and was clear about the results achieved every day. We got everyone focused on the goals, which reduced conflict and enabled cooperation. We dramatically improved our production through the processes listed and got the project back on track. When all was said and done, we didn't meet our initial estimate, but everyone involved knew how it might have turned out without a focus on results.

A TO Z APPLICATION

1. On a scale of 1–10, how do you rate on this trait. _____

2. Do you complete every job you start, or do you have a lot of unfinished projects sitting around? _____

   _____

   _____

   _____

3. If you were Rowan, what would you have done first when told to find Garcia? _____

   _____

   _____

   _____

4. How could you benefit from scoreboarding key metrics?_____

   _____

   _____

   _____

5. What action *will* you do differently to improve in this area? _

   _____

   _____

RESULTS-ORIENTATION JUMPSTART

- Read *A Message to Garcia*.
- Develop a goals plan for the next twelve months.
- Celebrate success.
- Keep score.
- Do things you are good at.

SELF -_____

Self-knowledge and self-improvement are very difficult for most people. It usually needs great courage and long struggle. —*Abraham Maslow*

self-knowl·edge - Having knowledge; conscious; cognizant; informed; alert / OPPOSITE - Oblivious; unaware; clueless; ignorant

———

It will come as no surprise to you that I am not a psychologist or a psychiatrist. Nor does staying at a Holiday Inn Express make me any smarter about this issue. What has helped me learn more is a whole lot of reading, study, and practice. The title of this chapter is "Self-" followed by a blank. There are actually several words we can put here, and I think there is a progression. A professional psychologist might disagree with my progression, but I think that is more a matter of semantics than concept.

It all starts with *self-awareness. Inc.* magazine wrote in 2007 that self-awareness was one of the least-discussed leadership competencies. Of course this was known long before *Inc.* wrote about it. Sun Tzu wrote, "If you know the enemy and know yourself, you will win a hundred battles." The fact that you are reading this book suggests you are interested in knowing more about yourself, and you work to become a more effective leader. Press on!

Do you know what is going on inside of you? Why do you feel the way you feel at any given moment? What are you good at? What are you not-so-good at? What do you fear, and why? You should know yourself better than anyone else. Most people do know themselves; they simply avoid the truth. John Gardner wrote in *Self-Renewal,* "More often than not, we don't want to know ourselves, don't want to depend on ourselves, don't want to live with ourselves. By middle life, most of us are accomplished fugitives from ourselves." The popularity of so-called reality TV shows, which people watch to escape their own lives, supports this. Former New York City Mayor Rudy Giuliani's opinion on the self-awareness? "I believe strongly that you should never be dishonest with yourself. You face your fear."

But why face your demons, fears, and flaws when you can just as easily deny them? Because in facing them, you can conquer them— and know that conquering a fear is sometimes not ridding yourself of it, but learning how to live with it. Philosopher Lao Tzu said, "Knowing others is intelligence. Knowing oneself is true wisdom." This quest for self-awareness is lifelong. With each layer of insight you develop, another one lies ready for discovery. Gaining awareness of right and wrong and acting in accordance with that knowledge is the first step on the journey.

When we have self-awareness, we can begin to develop self-esteem. As I noted at the outset, this is an incredibly complex concept that warrants further investigation. With that said, I prefer the two-pronged definition of self-esteem being comprised of *self-respect* ("I have value as a person") and *self-efficacy* ("I am capable and competent in my ability to think, decide, and act").

Self-esteem is a basic human need that only we can give to ourselves. We need food, clothing, and shelter, but others can provide that. We must develop our own sense of self-esteem. Without it, our development and potential is severely diminished. If it is low, we tend to be swallowed up by challenges and difficulties. Positive self-esteem is the immune system for our consciousness, maybe even for our souls. It provides resilience, our ability to get up when we get knocked down. Getting up makes us feel good. And when we feel good, we can accomplish more.

Self-esteem leads to *self-confidence*, that quality that organizes all our efforts and unifies them toward achievement of some great goal. Self-confidence instills in us the belief that we really can get what we want. It carries us and causes others to join with us. Self-confidence is mandatory in the knowledge and information economy. We are faced with almost limitless options wherever we look. Work presents us with the opportunity to make decisions all day long.

Nathaniel Branden, PhD, author of *The Power of Self-Esteem*, writes, "The greater the number of choices and decisions we need to make at a conscious level, the more urgent our need for self-esteem." When we are confident in our abilities, we are able to persevere when faced with tough choices and challenges. The very nature of perseverance, as noted earlier in "Endurance," means we will win more often than we lose. Brandon goes on to say that high self-esteem seeks the stimulation of demanding goals, while low self-esteem seeks the safety of the familiar and undemanding. In steadily choosing what we know and what is easy, we stunt the growth of our self-esteem and direct it away from success.

Unfortunately, self-esteem and all that stems from it is perishable. You must nourish and feed it. Words, deeds, articles, experience, positive self-talk—all must be put to work to keep your self-esteem oriented toward the positive. Conversely, you must avoid negative influences. With the underlying theme of television news being, "If it bleeds, it leads," you might do well to avoid such a negative impact on your psyche. And don't forget that the biggest impact on your self-esteem is your own self-talk. Be sure to make it positive.

Jeff Immelt, CEO of General Electric, is recognized for his thirst for continually getting better at what he does. He told an incoming class of MBAs at the University of Michigan, "The first part of leadership is an intense journey into yourself. It's a commitment and an intense journey into your soul . . . more than anything else, the burning desire inside me was to get the best out of what I could be and go on that journey."

Let's turn the discussion to emotional intelligence. While there is much debate on the nuances of the concept, there is less debate about the basic premise. A commonly accepted definition states that emotional intelligence is the innate potential to feel, use, communicate, recognize, remember, describe, identify, learn from, manage, understand, and explain emotions. Emotional intelligence is yet another tool in our toolbox to help us understand ourselves and to modulate ourselves to higher success.

The only way I can feel and use my own emotions to gain higher success is to have the self-awareness to be in touch with them, the self-esteem to know they have value, and the self-confidence to act on them. This may be one of the most difficult chapters to deal with since it demands brutal honesty. John Wooden said, "Be more concerned with your character than your reputation, because your character is what you *really* are while your reputation is merely what others *think* you are." Concern yourself with protecting your self-esteem, and your character will take care of itself.

The better you know and understand yourself, the better decisions you will make and the better results you will get. —Brian Tracy

SELF IN ACTION

Steve was a newly promoted regional manager at a highway construction company. He was recruited from a well-respected college with a degree in construction management. After spending his first season working in the field, he moved to the office where he rotated through several positions in estimating and operations.

After six years he was serving as a senior project manager, and after eight years he was the construction manager for the region. In these roles he was directly responsible for construction operations. He was also involved in interviewing candidates for jobs, but he was not involved in firing people. By all accounts, Steve was an outstanding employee, and after ten years he was promoted to regional manager.

In this new role he was responsible for aggregate operations and the manufacturing of hot mix asphalt. Though he worked closely with these areas as the construction manager, he was not involved in the daily operations of these divisions as a regional manager. He was also the ultimate authority on hiring and firing. This was new to him also.

Recognizing his own weakness in aggregates and manufacturing, he outlined an education plan that would allow him to learn as much as he could as quickly as he could. He asked for coaching from respected senior leaders outside of his chain of command, and he worked closely with his direct reports to learn from them and get their input on decisions. Steve knew what he didn't know and worked to gain knowledge about these areas. It didn't take long for him to have a working knowledge of the operations of all phases of his region.

He was also facing some challenges in holding people accountable. He had always been able to coach people and get the desired results, but one of his direct reports was not meeting the standard despite ongoing conversations about the need to improve performance. Steve created a 90-day action plan and met the employee who was below standard. Randy agreed that the plan was a good one and committed to working on improvement. Unfortunately, after 90 days there was little improvement. Steve met with Randy and shared his frustration and implemented another 90-day action plan. Again Randy made promises, but his performance did not change. In a final act of support, Steve crafted a 30-day action plan that only lasted for two weeks, because he terminated Randy after two weeks.

The total time involved here was almost ten months. Steve coached and cajoled, but Randy didn't get better. Shortly after terminating Randy, Steve took the DiSC profile. This assessment helps people understand some of their behavioral preferences. Steve learned that he had a profile that had an "overestimation of his ability to change people." Steve immediately recognized his time with Randy as confirmation of this statement. This new level of self-awareness was transformational for Steve. He learned to work with people more effectively but also to set milestones and deadlines and to hold to them.

This new self-awareness enabled him to act with confidence and to hold people accountable in a way he had never done before. His own performance and that of his direct reports improved, and his region was soon recognized as one of the best in the nation. Steve admits this wouldn't have happened had he not developed this new self-awareness.

A TO Z APPLICATION

1. On a scale of 1–10, how do you rate on this trait? _____

2. What causes you to be in a bad mood? _____

_____

_____

3. Can you admit you made a mistake? _____

_____

4. What specific action *will* you do to improve in this area? _____

_____

_____

SELF JUMPSTART

- Spend time with people who like you and care about you.
- Ignore (and stay away from) people who put you down or treat you badly.
- Do things that you enjoy or that make you feel good.
- Do things you are good at; reward yourself for your successes.
- Always do what you believe is right; be true to yourself and your values.

TIMELY

How does a project get to be a year behind schedule? One day at a time.
—Fred Brooks

time·ly - Occurring at a suitable time; seasonable; opportune; well timed / OPPOSITE - Late; tardy; unpunctual

———

At some point in your life you have probably heard that five minutes early is on time and on time is late. It isn't bad advice. The phrase "The early bird catches the worm" was first recorded in John Ray's *A collection of English proverbs* in 1670.

You must be on time. The phrase "better late than never" is poor advice for anyone aspiring to leadership. Being late sends several bad messages to people. I don't respect you, you don't matter, I am disorganized, and you cannot rely on me. None of those are very inspiring from a leadership perspective. It is tough to motivate followers when you are sending them the message that they don't matter and causing them to believe that you are not competent.

Being punctual, or on time, is only part of this. Another part of it is knowing when to take action, when to make your move. Leaders are savvy about timing and pick the right moment to take action. Have you ever walked into the office in the middle of the morning and asked, "Hey, is the boss in a good mood?" You have probably done this because you recognize the importance of timing.

The 1916 short story "Obvious Adams" shares five tests of obviousness, the fifth one being: Is the time ripe? Sometimes the time has passed and you should let the idea go. Sometimes the time just isn't right yet and you would do better to hold on to your idea. Ralph Waldo Emerson wrote in his *Journal*, "One of the cardinal virtues is timeliness." He also said, "The art of getting rich consists not in industry, much less in saving, but in a better order, in timeliness, in being at the right spot." I would add to Emerson and take action at that right spot.

Gorilla Glass was an idea that came before its time. A thin, flexible, and very strong glass product, it was invented in 1962 by Corning. Unfortunately, they could not find a viable use for it. So this wonderful product sat on the shelves for four decades. You probably use it a lot now. Many smart phones and other crystal displays feature it as the screen glass. Timing is everything.

One of the training programs we conduct at FireStarter is called Time Mastery. We believe leaders must be outstanding and ruthless in their use of time. To be any less puts you at a competitive disadvantage in the fast-paced, over-scheduled world we live in. We use an online assessment to help attendees understand their personal styles as they relate to various aspects of managing time. The assessment has twelve dimensions, with the final one being "team time." Others are attitudes, planning, goal setting, handling interruptions, and so on. There is one common theme across *every* group of managers who have taken the assessment. *Every* single group has ranked team time at the bottom of their list in importance. Team time is about changing the question from "What should I be doing now" to "What is the best use of our time?" This recognizes that top performance is a team effort requiring close synchronization of values and effort. When you are late to the meeting you called, you are in total ignorance of the concept of team time. When you don't get back to someone when you say you will, you are violating team time. This is a surefire way to tick people off and confirm a lack of leadership on your part.

The Rolling Stones made the Jerry Ragovoy tune "Time Is on My Side" a hit, but what works in music doesn't always work in the office. We might be better served here by the group Quantic who wrote "Time Is the Enemy". Perhaps Nike serves us best with "Just

Do It". Remember from results orientation that 90 percent of people said lack of time was the primary reason they did not exercise? Don't tell that to American artist Irwin Greenberg who said, "Don't say 'I haven't the time.' You have as much time every day as the great masters." There is a sobering thought for you. Why can some people get so much done and others so little? In our increasingly green eco-conscious world, one of the things we can't recycle is wasted time.

Broadcast journalists Jim Lehrer and Bernard Shaw, both former Marines, have each attributed the discipline of time learned in the corps to their success. Lenin and Stalin had people shot for being late. Okay, that might be a bit extreme, but you cannot stay on top of a situation if you are late. Mike Duke, CEO of Walmart, is known for tight adherence to his very full schedule. If a meeting is scheduled to end, it is not uncommon for him to get up and leave the meeting while someone is still talking. Of course, his employees have learned to be on time. He extends a similar focus to e-mail. At the end of the day he doesn't want any "carryovers"—he wants to have replied to all emails and phone messages by the end of the day. It helps him start with a clean slate the next day, but it also keeps things moving.

To me, one of the marks of a professional is to be on time. I cringe when we are running late as a family, and with two kids that happens. As a leader, it is simply not in my frame of reality to be late. Do circumstances arise that cause one to be late? Yes, but these must be few and far between. The more subtle but perhaps more important aspect of this trait is that sense of timing. Unfortunately, there is no formula to apply to develop this sense. Often we gain this over time by applying the lessons we learn and by understanding the people we are working with.

Punctuality is the stern virtue of men of business, and the graceful courtesy of princes. —*Edward G. Bulwer-Lytton*

TIMELINESS IN ACTION

The very first project that I ever worked on was a $50 million new construction student housing project for an academic institute involving a new client. Besides the typical hurdles that accompany a project of this size, the project had also been plagued by turnover at the highest level, including the construction manager and architect. My project team and I had to hit the ground running in order to keep up with the project schedule. We were forced to eliminate the preconstruction activities that are typically predecessors to a project this size.

While I wanted to start everything off on the right foot, the thought of trying to accomplish everything was just overwhelming. Seeing that I was overwhelmed and trying to please everyone, my manager gave me one piece of advice: Just be on time. He meant that I should not try to do everything at once but should meet my deadlines as they came. If I was going to miss a deadline, I needed to see that it got handled by somebody else or to let my boss know that we might miss it. Keeping my manager's advice in mind, I only committed to what I knew I could accomplish, and I prioritized my work in a way that allowed me to succeed as an individual and also as a member of the team.

During the two years that I was on that project, I was promoted to assistant project manager, and my team and I were able to successfully deliver a project that was on time and on budget—all due to the fact that everyone on the team knew their roles and we could rely on one another to accomplish the project at hand in a timely manner.

A TO Z APPLICATION

1. On a scale of 1–10, how do you rate on being timely ?_____

2. Are you consistently on time for all events?_____

  _____

3. List someone you know who exemplifies this trait: _____

  _____

4. On what things do you procrastinate? Why? _____

_____

_____

_____

_____

5. What action *will* you do to improve in this area?_____

_____

_____

_____

TIMELINESS JUMPSTART

- Cut 20 percent from your things-to-do list.
- Use a calendar system.
- Read *What Got You Here Won't Get You There.*
- Complete a time log and analyze your day/week.
- Be on time.

URGENT

Never lose your sense of urgency. Complacency, inertia, and procrastination are for also-rans. —Bill Brooks

ur·gent - The quality or condition of being urgent; pressing importance / OPPOSITE - Unimportant; unnecessary

———

The race is not always to the swift nor the battle to the strong. King Solomon in Ecclesiastes, who penned these words, may have been right, but I know for sure that the race cannot be won if you never start running. Leaders must have a bias for action. Leaders get the job done. A sense of urgency embodies a results orientation and is a primary part of being a role model.

We walk a fine line here as we talk about urgency. John Wooden, coach of UCLA basketball, was known for saying, "Be quick but don't hurry." Where is the line between quick and hurry? Perhaps only experience tells for sure, but what we do know is ours is a 24/7 society. Things move faster than they have ever moved before. While two hundred years ago a letter used to take three months to get to England, today it takes seconds.

How has our capacity to lead and process information changed to meet this increased pace? We are still human and only capable of so much, but the expectations are high. Woody Allen recognized this when he said, "It is clear the future holds opportunities—it also holds pitfalls. The trick will be to seize the opportunities, avoid the pitfalls, and get back home by 6:00." A. W. Clausen, former head of the World Bank, said, "I spend 60 percent of my time planning, 60 percent with people, and all other duties are completed with whatever time is left." In other words, his plate, like yours and mine, is full. Your inbox is never empty, so how do you get on top of things?

Having just talked about the importance of a sense of timing, you might think I am now contradicting myself by saying do it now, that one now is worth two laters. No, this is about doing the things that need to be done now. It relates directly to timing. The tongue in cheek, but all so accurate, Parkinson's Law tells us that work will expand to fill the time allotted to it. The best antidote to this is to get the work done.

Ulysses S. Grant was once asked how he could know he was right in a decision when he acted quickly on a great many of them.

Grant replied, "No, I am not [sure he was always right] but in war anything is better than indecision. We must decide. If am wrong we shall soon find out and can do the other thing. But to not decide wastes both time and money and may ruin everything." Meetings are wonderful to have when you want to avoid making a decision. They allow weak managers to analyze and discuss. Done well, they lead to a consensus decision, but all too often the same things get discussed the next time with no action taken.

Indecision is the rage in corporate America today, because to decide is to risk being wrong, and to be wrong invites scrutiny and scrutiny can be uncomfortable and, possibly, career ending. CEOs can surround themselves with vice presidents who counsel and advise to protect the CEO from making a bad decision. Procrastination then becomes the order of the day and becomes ingrained in the culture of the organization. Making decisions, however, sends the message we have a bias for action, and we are moving forward. The leader who makes a mistake but continues to make decisions, most of them good, will be far more successful than the one who becomes paralyzed by inaction. Most people reading this are not CEOs, so if you don't take action, everyone will know it is you not doing it!

Harvard professor John Kotter, in *A Sense of Urgency*, identifies the single biggest factor to successful change as the inability to create a true sense of urgency. That would suggest a communications issue as much as an urgency issue. H. Jackson Brown said, "You must take action now that will move you towards your goals. Develop a sense of urgency in your life."

In 2010 Sergio Marchionne became the CEO of Fiat-Chrysler. He had already succeeded with Fiat and now his focus was on Chrysler. In a counterintuitive approach, he centralized all decision making. While this has the potential to create bottlenecks, he avoids this by making decisions immediately. His managers have access to him 24/7, and when they call or e-mail him he makes decisions in minutes or seconds. Ralph Gilles, who has worked at Chrysler since 1992, summed up the impact, "We have urgency and quick decision making, and the bureaucracy is completely gone."

At the corporate level, Noel Tichy talks about return on time. Those waiting for the pace to slow down so they can catch up and get back on track will be waiting a long time. As evidenced by Marchionne, those days are long gone. Tichy says leaders with a return on time mindset are always thinking about getting the most out of every minute. Andy Grove of Intel fame was a fanatic about starting meetings on time. He pointed out that stealing $2000 worth of office equipment would not be tolerated. Nor would stealing time.

Some people are historians and futurists, I prefer to be a nowist. Rather than look back longingly at the good old days or whittle away the time hoping for that better future, I take action now to capitalize on what I learned in the past to move toward what I want for the future. There is a wonderful book on meditation by Jon Kabat-Zinn, *Wherever You Go, There You Are: Mindfulness Meditation in Everyday Life*. The author tells us meditation is important because it brings about a state of "mindfulness," a condition of "being" rather than "doing" during which you pay attention to the moment rather than the past, the future, or the multitudinous distractions of modern life. In other words, you are in the now.

It is a simple fact. Leaders (and winners) have a bias for action. They not only know what needs to be done, but they get started on getting it done, which, of course, enables them to actually get it done. Forget completion dates; how about start dates? Cultivate a sense of urgency, and you will be planting the seeds of success.

Without a sense of urgency, desire loses its value. —*Jim Rohn*

URGENT IN ACTION

Last year over a holiday weekend we were trenching in the downtown core. The crew had followed all safety procedures, and they were fully up to standard. A cyclist cut through the lane closure and fell into a trench. He was slightly injured.

As soon as I got the call, I asked for pictures to be sent to me to review. I called our senior field folks to a meeting on the next

Monday. We all sat down and went through the incident and the pictures. We concluded that although we were following procedures, we needed to improve. The senior field staff and crew leaders reviewed the pictures, went back to the site to inspect it, and worked to improve our procedure for protecting the public.

By the end of the day we came up with a new procedure for worksite protection. We had buy-in from everyone because we all developed it. The new standard was rolled out to all our field staff the next day.

Today we have one of the best worksite protection plans in the city. This includes better signage, fencing, training, documentation, and our own temporary traffic control manual. It was important, and we got it done immediately.

A TO Z APPLICATION

1. On a scale of 1–10, how do you rate on urgency? _____

2. What project do you need to get started on, now? _____

   _____

   _____

3. List someone you know who exemplifies this trait: _____

   _____

4. Why do you think you procrastinate? _____

_____

_____

_____

5. What action *will* you do to improve in this area? _____

_____

_____

URGENCY JUMPSTART

- Develop a goals plan—then use it.
- Read *The One Minute Manager Meets the Monkey*.
- Return calls and e-mail within twelve hours.
- Set start dates and end dates.

VISIONARY

Vision is the art of seeing what is invisible to others. —*Jonathan Swift*

vi·sion·ar·y - a person of unusually keen foresight / OPPOSITE - Myopic; shortsighted, plodding

————

Just about any book on leadership will have something on the importance of looking ahead. The problem, however, is that the discussion of vision often gets murky. As I said in *No Yelling*, the two basic questions we want to address with vision are, "Where are we going?" and "Why are we going there?" Yet they are the ones least frequently answered.

When we talk about vision, we simply mean an orientation toward the future. Sure, the idea can be somewhat abstract, as noted by Swift in the opening quotation, or it can be much more pragmatic. John Kotter, noted scholar on leadership and change, says,

"Leaders establish the vision for the future and set the strategy for getting there; they cause change. They motivate and inspire others to go in the right direction and they, along with everyone else, sacrifice to get there." Although he doesn't tell us where the vision he refers to comes from, he is sure of the leader's responsibility to make it happen.

And how does the leader accomplish this? By creating a picture in his or her mind of what they want to happen, and then getting other people to see and buy into that picture, too. The more clarity and detail, the better. People who succeed in the world see themselves succeeding. Golfers actually see the ball flying to the hole in their minds' eye before they hit the ball. Civil War Navy Admiral David Farragut, when asked if he was prepared for defeat, said, "I certainly am not. Any man who is prepared for defeat is half-defeated before he commences." He also uttered those classic words, "Damn the torpedoes, full speed ahead!" Defeat was simply not part of his vision of the future.

Not long ago, business pundits talked of strategic planning and the importance of looking three to five years down the road. However, in the economic meltdown of 2009, this thinking was challenged as firms struggled to look three to five *months* ahead. Admittedly, many strategic plans took a hit, and even more required a rewrite. But firms that kept an eye on the future fared better in the recovery. In 2008, as the housing market cratered, Home Depot was already looking toward recovery. Even though the economy was still in freefall, the leaders at Home Depot were making plans to address some of the company's most pressing needs, identified in customer complaints. They implemented a number of improvements that enabled them to increase earnings on lower-level sales. I have worked with other companies who can report similar success as they make changes with an eye to the future.

Jim Collins and Jerry I. Porras wrote *Built to Last: Successful Habits of Visionary Companies*. They endorse a "five whys" conversation to help you uncover and understand your core purpose, which some would call your vision. Pioneered at Toyota, this process helps leaders dig deep when considering a problem. Five isn't a fixed number; the concept suggests you have to keep asking to get to the real answer.

It remains for the leader to keep peering ahead, to keep asking why. But that's not enough. As we saw in Execution, the leader must develop the plan and work to make it happen. Futurist Joel Barker underscores this bias for action (urgency): "Vision without action is a dream. Action without vision is simply passing the time. Action with vision is making a positive difference." When you put energy into vision you are beginning to reach people on an emotional, maybe even spiritual, level. It gives them something to commit to.

Howard Schultz built Starbucks on vision but over time the firm drifted from it. The drift was big enough that Schultz left his role as Chairman and resumed his position as CEO. Shortly after his return he closed every store for three hours of training for every employee. He then brought every manager, 10,000 of them, to New Orleans for a meeting in which he reminded them, face to face, of the vision and the importance of living their values in fulfilling the vision. Shultz says, "If we hadn't had New Orleans, we wouldn't have turned the company around. It was real, it was truthful, it was about leadership."

As an employee, I want to know that my employer has a plan. It gives me a sense of security and hope for a future that includes me as a fully employed member of a team. This is not to say that employees will blindly embrace their leader's vision, whatever it may be. Legendary management guru Peter Drucker commented: "Leadership is not magnetic personality—that can just as well be a glib tongue. It is not making friends and influencing people—that is flattery. Leadership is lifting a person's vision to higher sights, the raising of a person's performance to a higher standard, the building of a personality beyond its normal limitations."

In other words, you need to work to get employees to see the future, accept your concept of it, and then work to achieve it. This is a challenge in an economy in which so many workers live paycheck to paycheck. "People underestimate their capacity for change" wrote noted business researcher John Porter. "There is never a right time to do a difficult thing. A leader's job is to help people have vision of their potential."

We didn't go to the moon because President John F. Kennedy thought bringing back rocks from space would be good for science (although he might have). We went to the moon because he, the leader of our country, laid it out as a grand endeavor worthy of this great nation. It was an inspiring, lofty vision that challenged us and people rallied behind it. Martin Luther King didn't simply think about civil rights. He dreamed big and changed the way our society thought about race.

Success does come to those who think about the future. Research confirms that successful people spend at least fifteen minutes every day thinking about what they are going to do in the future and what they can do in the present to improve their lives. How is that possible when we are all so busy? This confirms the power of vision. It is worth the effort to create and sustain because it energizes people and steers them toward their goals.

A great leader's courage to fulfill his vision comes from passion, not position. —John Maxwell

VISION IN ACTION

Founded in 1982 as an open-shop contractor in Boston, Suffolk Construction has risen to number thirty-one on the ENR list of Top 400 Contractors with $1.7 billion in revenue. CEO John Fish is the man with the plan who has passionately built the firm from its humble roots.

From day one he had a vision of creating something that would stand the test of time and be one of the best. His strong work ethic sets a solid foundation for the firm and he looks for employees who are driven to succeed. Early on he hired marketing and sales professionals to be the face of Suffolk, with the aim of creating a national brand. While this may have been his unstated vision in the first decade or two, the vision of Suffolk is now codified in the Suffolk Pyramid.

The Suffolk website describes it this way: "The pyramid, a recognizable symbol of strength and stability, is the perfect symbol of Suffolk's corporate strategy. Our core values serve as a strong foundation that supports the rest of the Suffolk Pyramid. Our strategies, built on top of our foundation of core values, act as "stepping stones" to our company's greater purpose and represent the direction we need to follow to become a great company. Our vision statement resides at the Suffolk summit and represents the company we are striving to become. The vision of Suffolk is Building Relationships By Exceeding Expectations."

Of course, those are just words on paper that may not look like much. But when you consider the successful growth Suffolk has enjoyed over the years, it is easy to see that the vision of John Fish has been the driving force. Fish isn't content to be a successful contractor; he wants Suffolk to be known as one of the country's great corporations.

A TO Z APPLICATION

1. On a scale of 1 – 10, how do you rate on vision? _____

   _____

2. Do you have a personal mission or vision that you refer to on a regular basis? _____

   _____

   _____

3. List someone you know who exemplifies this trait: _____

   _____

4. What specific things can you do to improve in this area? _____

   _____

   _____

5. How do you communicate your vision and plans to your team?
   Do they get it? _____

   _____

   _____

VISION JUMPSTART

- Write the speech they will make the day you retire.
- Make your bucket list.
- Conduct a "five whys" exercise for the vision you have for yourself.
- Develop a vision for your company or work group.
- Read *Switch*.

WILLING

The extent and complexity of the problem does not matter as much as does the willingness to solve it. —Ralph Marston

wil·ing - Disposed to; consenting; inclined; ready / OPPOSITE - Reluctant; against; opposed to

In 1640 people said, "To him that will, ways are not wanting." Today we say, "Where there's a will, there's a way." Both imply that simply wanting is not enough. We must *actively move* toward acquiring or achieving that which we want. This willingness opens us to possibilities and allows our minds to being working on solutions.

Associate professor of art criticism and theory at the University of Nevada, Las Vegas, David Hickey differentiates between "looky-loos" and "participants." In his book *Air Guitar: Essays on Art and Democracy*, he describes looky-loos as those folks who don't really *live* life. They display little passion and even less eagerness to step up and take action. Participants, on the other hand, are those who get things done—they are the movers and shakers in society.

Theodore Roosevelt would compare them to "the man in the arena." The one "marred by dust and sweat and blood, who strives valiantly, who errs, who comes short again and again, because there is no effort without error and shortcoming; but who, in the end, knows the triumph of high achieving."

Wanting is about reclining in your easy chair and running your mouth about what's wrong with things. Being willing is about making a decision and leaning forward toward the edge of your chair. Of course, participation is about getting out of the chair and into the arena.

But you must be willing before you can participate. This is where *initiative* comes in. Another Marine Corps leadership trait, it is defined as "taking action in the absence of orders"—a willingness to act in the face of uncertainty.

If you Google *willing* or *willingness*, you will get a lot of hits that deal with recovery from addiction and a few more on religion. These aren't bad places to pause, as many of them offer a step-by-step approach to become more open to possibilities.

Perhaps participants in *USA Today's* Family Fitness Challenge would do well to embrace these steps. Asked why they were not more physically active, their replies included:

- Our biggest challenge is laziness and procrastination.
- We watch TV after dinner.
- We are too tired at the end of the day.

In other words, they simply weren't *willing* to get moving.

Inventor Ronald Riley commented that many of our great American industrial firms were initially run by inventors who were willing to take big risks by introducing new inventions. With success and middle age, the companies became more rigid and less willing to take chances. Once stagnation set in, the companies lost the desire to innovate and were unwilling to take *any* risk. And, as you know, the refusal to take risks is a sure way to cripple a business.

Willingness is a key to creativity and to achieving what is possible. Rhodes Scholar Edward de Bono wrote, "One very important aspect of motivation is the willingness to stop and look at things that no one else has bothered to look at. This simple process of focusing on things that are normally taken for granted is a powerful source of creativity." And it won't happen unless you are willing.

Speaker and author Joe Calloway submits that it may seem counterintuitive, but, in order to succeed, you must be willing to fail. Almost everyone will agree that their organization must be innovative to stay competitive. Innovative means being the first to do something, and being the first to do something means there are no guarantees of success. Innovative organizations understand that, in trying new ideas, there comes the risk of making mistakes. They also understand that mistakes are seldom fatal. In fact, they can be great sources of new information. You can fix the problem and learn a lot.

Business guru, the late Peter Drucker, once said that consistently successful businesses are led by people who are "willing to make courageous decisions." Where does courage come into play? It comes in the willingness to let go of what we are used to and the assumptions that we have made about what we do and how we do it.

If you are not willing, you are not open. But being open means admitting that you might not know something, and many managers have a hard time with that. If management is black and white, leadership is about the gray areas. Thriving in the gray areas means coming to terms with imprecision. The creative person with an open and willing mind looks further and is flexible and able to adapt as a situation changes. A lack of flexibility and an unwillingness to be open to the possibilities is not a success strategy. In fact, it's just the opposite.

Where the willingness is great, the difficulties cannot be great.
—Niccolo Machiavelli

WILLINGNESS IN ACTION

Nikki started at O'Neil Construction, an ENR Top 200 general contractor, as an office manager. It was a clerical position with lots of filing, data entry, and phone answering. Nikki excelled and, over time, it was apparent that she had far more to offer the company. Eventually, she was approached with the idea of becoming a project engineer (PE). The PE position can be highly technical, usually staffed by college graduates with engineering degrees, which Nikki did not have. She was told the hours would likely be long, and she would be required to take some extension courses and work far from home at times. She agreed to give it a shot.

Within a couple years, Nikki had proven herself successful enough to be asked to speak at our annual PE training session. Terrified is probably too strong a word to use to describe her reaction, but just barely. Upon being convinced that she had the ability to bring value, she agreed to give it a shot.

Nikki has become one of the most respected PEs in our company, loves her job, and is looking at a promotion to project manager someday soon. She told me, after presenting at the training session, that speaking to one's peers is one of the most rewarding things she's ever done. Neither task came easy. Nikki has worked very hard at becoming an engineer who is a key component to her project's success. She has also described to me her speech preparation formula—it's not quick or easy. In both cases, especially with the presentation, Nikki stepped out of her comfort zone— way out. But she was willing to consider the proposal and willing to make the difficult choice. She's glad she did both.

A TO Z APPLICATION

1. On a scale of 1–10, how do you rate on willingness? _____

2. Is your glass half full or half empty? _____
   _____
   _____

3. List someone you know who exemplifies willingness: _____
   _____

4. What old baggage are you still carrying around? Is this helping your attitude, or do you need to let it go? _____
   _____
   _____
   _____

5. What action *will* you do to improve in this area?_____
   _____
   _____

WILLINGNESS JUMPSTART

- Say yes.

- Be open to unexpected outcomes.

- Practice mindfulness—read *Wherever You Go, There You Are.*

X GENERATION
(AND OTHERS)

It's hard for me to get used to these changing times. I can remember when the air was clean and sex was dirty. —George Burns

gen·er·ation - a group of individuals, most of whom are the same approximate age, have similar ideas, problems, attitudes, etc. / OPPOSITE - Diversity; dissimilar

———

The concept of the generation gap is not a new one. It's a discrepancy in attitudes, values, lifestyles, economic opportunities, and other areas between people of significant age difference. Every generation has its own distinct attitudes, behaviors, and motivational "buttons" that develop as a result of the times in which they grew up. And the characteristics of each generation often differ from those of the generations preceding them, leading to lack of understanding between all concerned. The resulting fallout regularly causes a major drain on productivity in the workplace. John Molidor, PhD, notes this fallout in his book *Psycho Generations: How Each Generation Drives The Other Crazy And What You Can Do About It.*

In case you are not familiar with the various generations in our society today, below is a listing of recent generations for individuals born in the United States. Dates are approximate, as recognized by demographers. *Caution: Stereotyping and erroneous generalities are possible when you dump a few hundred million people into just a few buckets.*

> 2000/2001–Present—New Silent Generation or Generation Z
> 1980–2000—Millennials or Generation Y
> 1965–1980—Generation X
> 1946–1964—Baby Boom
> 1925–1945—Silent Generation
> 1900–1924—GI Generation

This is the first time in our history where the generations are so distinctly different. If you lived in the United States in 1820, you would have grown up in a primarily agricultural society. The same could be said for 1920. Things didn't change much in that 100-year period, so differences of opinion weren't that great—or divisive. Most people still worked on the family farm. But the twentieth century saw a rate of change unlike the nation had ever seen before. Technology, mobility, speed, family dynamics, economics, and much more truly do make the generations different. Your challenge as a leader is to understand and navigate those differences. Then you can steer clear of misunderstandings between you and your workers and among your workers themselves.

It would take too much space to fully cover the generational differences, but here is a brief summary to get you started:

PERSONAL AND LIFESTYLE CHARACTERISTICS BY GENERATION				
	Veterans (1920–1945)	Baby Boomers (1946–1964)	Generation X (1965–1980)	Generation Y (1981–2000)
Core Values	Respect for authority Conforms Discipline	Optimism Involvement	Skepticism Fun Informality	Realism Confidence Extreme fun Social
Family	Traditional Nuclear	Disintegrating	Latch-key kids	Merged families
Education	A dream	A birthright	A way to get there	An incredible expense
Communication Media	Rotary phones One-on-one Write a memo	Touch-tone phones Call me anytime	Cell phones Call me only at work	Internet Picture phones E-mail Instant Messaging
Attitudes about Money	Put it away Pay cash	Buy now, pay later	Cautious Conservative Save, save, save	Earn to spend

WORKPLACE CHARACTERISTICS			
	Veterans **(1920–1945)**	**Baby Boomers** **(1946–1964)**	**Generation X** **(1965–1980)**	**Generation Y** **(1981–2000)**
Work Ethic and Values	Hard work Respect Authority Sacrifice Duty before fun Adhere to rules	Workaholics Work efficiently Crusading causes Personal fulfillment Desire quality Question authority	Eliminate the task Self-reliance Want structure and direction Skeptical	What's next Multitasking Tenacity Entrepreneurial Tolerant Goal oriented
Work Is...	An obligation	An exciting adventure	A difficult challenge A contract	A means to an end Fulfillment
Leadership Style	Directive Command- and-control	Consensual Collegial	Everyone is the same Challenge others Ask why	TBD
Interactive Style	Individual	Team player Loves to have meetings	Entrepreneur	Participative
Communications	Formal memo	In-person	Direct Immediate	E-mail Voice mail
Feedback and Rewards	No news is good news Satisfaction in a job well done	Don't appreciate it Money Title Recognition	Sorry to inter- rupt, but how am I doing? Freedom is the best reward	Whenever I want it, at the push of a button Meaningful work
Messages That Motivate	Your experience is respected	You are valued You are needed	Do it your way Forget the rules	You will work with other bright, creative people
Work and Family Life	Nev'er the twain shall meet	No balance Work to live	Balance	Balance

Here's the bottom line: You are *you*, with your own attitudes and beliefs. And that's fine. The people around you have *their* own attitudes and beliefs, too, and those are fine. What is wrong is judging others and devaluing their possible contributions because their beliefs do not match yours.

Jim Turley, CEO of Ernst and Young, noted that the top three things young people care about today are the same three things baby boomers are looking for: learning and growth opportunities, being in an organization they trust and that offers a career path, and having flexibility in their lives. What is very clear is that people today want more control over their lives . . . they want to be treated like professionals from day one, trusted to get the job done. I often hear managers complain about being nothing more than glorified babysitters. I contend this is a self-fulfilling statement. If you think your employees are babies, you will treat them as such. It logically follows they will then act as such. Within each generation are people who want to excel. They want to be led, and it is up to you to lead them.

In *Generations at Work*, Zemke, Raines, and Filipczak present the ACORN principle for leading across generations.

1. Accommodate differences,

2. Create workplace choices,

3. Operate from a sophisticated management style,

4. Respect competence and initiative, and

5. Nourish retention.

"Different" is not a question of good or bad. It is simply . . . different. If you accept that leadership is about building positive relationships with people, then it will not be difficult for you to accept your responsibility to get to know each of your people. It may be harder to get to know some than others, but the final outcome will make it worth the effort.

There was no respect for youth when I was young, and now that I am old, there is no respect for age—I missed it coming and going! —J.B. Priestly

X GENERATION IN ACTION

The clash of generations in the workplace continues, but there are firms who have learned to work through these challenges.

Baby boomers raised on black-and-white television screens have a hard time comprehending how millennials raised on three screens (TV, computer, and handheld device) can get anything done while looking at all three. They also don't understand, nor appreciate, having a conversation with someone wearing ear buds. At best this is rude, at worst it will mean concepts lost in translation. One firm created IPod-free zones. These devices are simply not permitted in common areas. Another firm created IPod-free times. From 6 to 9 AM, when many field people and route drivers were in the office, IPods were not permitted. After 9 AM they could be worn.

Technology presents other challenges. Employees checking cell phones while on a construction job site not only lowers productivity, but it is also a safety issue. Some contractors have instituted policies prohibiting cell phone use unless the crew is on a break.

Mentoring and reverse mentoring are the most fertile ground in this area. Many firms have instituted formal programs where senior leaders are paired with promising up-and-comers. There are many variations to these programs, but the common thread of enhancing communication and mutual understanding remains.

In some firms newer employees are coaching and mentoring senior employees. For example, younger employees tend to be more comfortable with technology. One top drywall firm paired a junior estimator who had not quite two years on the job with the chief estimator to field and implement a new program for on-screen takeoffs. This combined approach enabled the firm to field the software more rapidly and realize a faster payback on the investment. In rolling out the software, they worked together to teach all estimators. Not only are estimators 35 percent faster when doing takeoffs, the firm is 1.63 percent more accurate on materials costs for drywall jobs. This has proven to be the margin of victory on several large projects.

Manganaro Construction is a top drywall and masonry firm operating on the eastern seaboard. They have done a good job over the years of recruiting interns and later hiring them. Many of these interns-turned-project engineers have gone on to become successful project managers and senior project managers. However, in 2008 and 2009, they noticed that the quality of the new engineers was going down. While they looked great on paper with a high GPA and all the things you would "want" in a new hire, the attrition rate was at an all time high for this group. The data was clear, and Manganaro took action. They reviewed the profile for a project engineer and updated it to reflect some of the changing values and motivators of the Gen Y graduates coming into their firm. They used assessments to learn more about what drove each candidate, and they were able to make better hires with this new process. They made other changes to the hiring and onboarding process, and initial data suggests these moves are right on target. Different generation, different approach.

A TO Z APPLICATION

1. On a scale of 1–10, how do you rate on understanding different generations? _____

2. How well do you work across generations? _____
   _____

3. What about each of the generations do you admire? _____
   _____
   _____
   _____

4. What about each of the generations ticks you off? _____
   _____
   _____
   _____

5. Who, from a different generation, can you get to know better?
   _____
   _____

X GENERATION JUMPSTART

- Get to know someone from a generation you have a hard time with.
- Remember what it was like when you were young—then get over it.
- Read *Maslow on Management*.

YIELD

You got to know when to hold 'em, know when to fold 'em, Know when to walk away, know when to run. —Kenny Rogers, *The Gambler*

yield - To give way to influence, entreaty, argument; cease resisting / OPPOSITE - Steadfast; obstinate; unyielding

——————

Kenny Rogers goes on to explain in the song, "Ev'ry gambler knows that the secret to survivin' is knowin' what to throw away and knowing what to keep." As a leader, you face challenges every day. Some are easily overcome; others, not so easily. The art is in knowing the difference. Not knowing can deliver a Pyrrhic victory—that is a win *technically*, but at a devastating cost. In fact, the triumph sets the victor back so far that it may well erase any hope of future success. The phrase is named after King Pyrrhus of Epirus, whose army suffered irreplaceable casualties while defeating the Romans in the Pyrrhic

War (280–279 BC). After the final battle, King Pyrrhus is said to have remarked that one more such victory would utterly undo him.

Clearly there are some causes worth fighting for. But there are many worth *not* fighting for. In Shakespeare's *Henry IV*, Falstaff tells us, "The better part of valour is discretion; in which the better part I have saved my life." Certainly I am not endorsing cowardice here. Simply, as my friend Grady says, "If they ping, I don't have to pong." Neither do you.

Many a career has been ruined on so-called *principle*. I have found that when people say things like, "I don't care about the money/title/promotion; it's the principle of the thing!" it's not the "principle" at all. Ethics and integrity are important, and we should uphold and abide by them. We should not, however, hide behind them. As Stanley Baldwin, three-time prime minister of the United Kingdom wrote, "I would rather be an opportunist and float than go to the bottom with my principles round my neck."

In June 2009 Timberland CEO Jeff Swartz was bombarded with e-mail from activists concerned about the deforestation of Brazilian forests. (Much of that land gets converted to pasture for cattle. Some of those hides, in turn, become shoe leather for Timberland.) Greenpeace was demanding that something be done. The easy solution would have been for Swartz to get out of Brazil. Only 7 percent of Timberland's leather came from there. But Swartz was also angry. The company was committed to the environment. It had planted one million trees in China. This campaign wasn't really fair, considering his firm's record. He could have gone on the offensive and rebutted the claims. Instead, he yielded to reason and considered the facts of the claims made by Greenpeace. He found they had some merit, so he proceeded to explore the possibilities. From positive engagement with those who e-mailed him, to closer cooperation with suppliers and Brazilian authorities, Timberland earned praise from Greenpeace for its response.

There are other things you don't have to do "just because." You don't have to come up with the best idea. You don't always have to be the one with the plan, the solution. While you may have a very good plan or idea in mind, it may serve your company's needs better to run with someone else's. Why not use the idea from one of your people if the outcome is likely to be similar? Certainly there are times your plan will clearly be the better option, but not always. Not using your people's plan tells them you don't think them capable. Further, it says you don't trust them. Talk about demotivating!

Then sometimes you simply have to get out of the way. Your presence may be appreciated, but there may not be much value you can add. General James Conway, USMC, traveled to Afghanistan about every four months during his time as commandant. While his presence surely motivated the troops, it also distracted them. He learned during his command time in Iraq that visiting too often was a burden. Better to simply stay out of the way.

Sometimes you may not be the best person for the job. That is not to say you can't do the job and do it well; there may be people out there who can do it better. This is true at FireStarter. I love speaking to groups. Speeches and training are my passions. Coaching? Not so much. I do it and I do it well, but, given the choice, I would give a speech. Steve Brooks is our lead executive coach. He is truly gifted in the area of developing people, and he is very effective. Couple his excellence with my preferences, and I am happy to yield to him on matters related to coaching. Together we make a great team. Were I not to yield, that might not be the case. Certainly our clients would not be getting maximum value.

The concept of losing the battle to win the war is not new. Sun Tzu wrote of this in the sixth century BC. In fact, it is one of the keys to success for leaders. Time simply doesn't allow you to do everything you think you need to do. Your inbox is full, and there are people who don't see things your way. In an ideal world, you would address all of these things. Reality is different. Sometimes you need to know when to walk away.

We lost the American colonies because we lacked the statesmanship to know the right time and the manner of yielding what is impossible to keep. —Elizabeth II

YIELD IN ACTION

Berghammer Construction is a commercial general contractor in southeast Wisconsin. The firm has a reputation as one of the top general contractors in the region. President Leif Nesheim has guided this successful growth. I asked him if he has "yielded" as a leader? His answer was quick but firm. "Yield? Yes. Not the easiest thing to do but . . . yes, many times."

He went on to explain his perspective. "One of my primary jobs as a leader at Berghammer is to grow our people into leaders. Certainly coaching and mentoring is one method. However, letting my people learn through experience is another. There are times I have let significant issues work their way through our management team without taking an active stance in the conversation. Although I wanted to jump in and I knew, full well, the desired outcome I was looking for, I stood aside. I also know that if team members are going to learn, they benefit most from hands-on experience. So I let the internal decision process run its own course. One time, well after a positive resolution, one of our execs asked me if I would have stepped in along the way. His phrase was something like "would I have let the ship hit the rocks"? Of course not. As the 'Captain,' I knew where the rocks were and would intervene, if necessary. I think all good leaders do, but I think all great leaders will let the ship get close to the rocks and let the crew steer the ship clear. The easier decision is for me to take the helm and jump in. But this would not allow others to feel their way through the process of making a good decision. The ultimate payoff in stepping aside is the increasing capacity of our leadership team."

Leif noted that the concept of yielding extends beyond employees to clients. He related a time where a client was dissatisfied with a project manager's performance.

Upon further review, it was clear that this was a clash of personalities. The job was ahead of schedule and on budget, but the owner requested the project manager be removed from the project. This was a tough decision. The project was 67 percent complete, and the project manager had a total understanding of the job and its history. Nesheim made the decision to "yield" to the wishes of the client. However, he created a best-case scenario as they moved forward. The project manager remained involved with the nonclient contact aspects of the job. He continued to communicate with subcontractors and with our internal field staff. Leif stepped in to attend weekly job meetings. They maintained management continuity on the job while fulfilling the client request.

Nesheim explained, "We would have been well within our rights to leave the project manager on the job, but that isn't our way. We don't fight clients, we work with them. And yes, we incurred some cost, and I invested some extra time on the final third of that project. Was it worth it? Absolutely. We have built two more projects for the client, and the relationship is stronger than ever."

YIELD IN ACTION (BONUS)

An ENR top 200 general contractor had a project manager working on a large project at one of the big semiconductor firms. The project manager had a good track record. We were executing a new type of contract for us and the firm. The particular site had done all their own contract management in the past and didn't like us being shoved down their throat by purchasing. The site was experimenting with a homegrown project administration system. The project manager was caught in the middle of politics, a new contract, experimental software, a customer team that didn't like anything we did or said, and many other issues. People onsite were covering their butts thinking they were going to lose their jobs. Our project manager got blamed for every error, every problem, everything that went awry.

After things got really nasty, I had a heart-to-heart with the customer rep and purchasing. I pulled the project manager off the job, even though everyone agreed the failures were on all sides. I put in a new project manager and let him get his feet wet for a month or so and then brought in a consultant with expertise in facilitating meetings with a dysfunctional team and angry people. Within a couple of months, the customer gave us a good report. Thumbs up! Within a year, it was one of our happiest sites for that customer.

I know there are some people who would say we were not loyal to our first project manager, but this wasn't about him; it was about a project relationship. Had we dismissed him, we would be in the wrong, but we put him on a new project and he continued to do great work for us.

A TO Z APPLICATION

1. On a scale of 1–10, how do you rate on this trait? _____

2. Do you have a hard time giving way? Why or why not? _____

   _____

   _____

   _____

3. List someone you know who exemplifies the ability to yield:

   _____

4. Have you ever
   fought for something "on principle"? _____

   _____

   _____

5. What action *will* you do to improve in this area?_____

_____

_____

YIELD JUMPSTART

- Recognize you don't have to win every battle. Some simply don't need to be fought.
- Ask yourself if that fight was worth giving a piece of your life to.
- Delegate.
- You can be happy or right.
- Read *The Lost Art of Listening*.

ZEAL

Experience shows that success is due less to ability than to zeal. The winner is he who gives himself to his work, body and soul. —*Charles Buxton*

zeal - Fervor for a person, cause, or object; eager desire or endeavor; enthusiastic diligence; ardor / OPPOSITE - Apathy; indifference; lethargy

———

How bad do you want it? No matter what it is, for you to get it, you have to want it. Enthusiasm is a Marine Corps leadership trait. The corps defines it as the display of sincere interest in and exuberance in the performance of duty. No false motivation; just pure fervor for the cause.

If you don't care, neither will your employees. In *Leadership Is a Relationship* by Kouzes and Posner, one of the most desirable qualities in a leader is that he or she be "inspirational." The ability of a supervisor to encourage and excite their team is important. And I think the best way to do this is through their drive for what they do—their *zeal* or *passion*. It is important to note I am not talking about phony cheerleading. Your employees can detect insincerity instantly. And in addition to them resenting it, they will think you shallow and manipulative.

Think about football coaches. There is the Landry-Shula-Dungy-even-keeled style, and then there is the Ditka-Cowher-Gruden-volcanic style. Both styles are right—as is everything in between. But this isn't about style; it is about zeal or passion. Bill Walsh, coach of the San Francisco 49ers answered a question about his strengths this way, "I have a passion for what I do." No doubt each of these men was fervently enthusiastic about the game; their players responded to their passion. Employees are no different.

Consider your introduction of two initiatives. The first you explain with the energy and support you would have for a root canal. The second you describe with the zeal and passion you have for your favorite hobby. Which one has the best chance of succeeding? Which one has *no* chance of succeeding? You know the answer. Leadership is not a popularity contest. Leaders face challenges on even the best of days. More often they are running an uphill race to implement change in the face of employee resistance and economic uncertainty. Who motivates the motivator? The better question is *what* motivates the motivator. Passion is the answer.

Scandinavian poet Edith Sodergran says, "The inner fire is the most important thing mankind possesses." FireStarter Speaking and Consulting, the name of my firm, is all about creating that fire in the belly to help people lead themselves, their people, and their firms more effectively. I get a lot of sideways looks when people hear the name of my company. But when I explain what it means, they always nod in approval because they know that inner fire, passion, is a key to success. You will never lose energy doing something you love to do. I love what I do. Like most work, it is tiring. But unlike many jobs, it is not tiresome.

Leon Leonwood (you would know him as LL) Bean felt the same way about his work. He started LL Bean in 1912. His letter in the 1962 catalog, the fiftieth anniversary catalog, thanked customers. It then went on to say, "I have always greatly enjoyed hunting and fishing and can honestly say it has been a pleasure helping others enjoy these wonderful sports." He died five years later at the age of ninety-four. He was active in the business until the very end—fifty-five years of passionate leadership of a company providing a product he stood behind to clients who trusted him. The growth of the firm during that period is a testimony to the impact of passion.

We all know of Zig Ziglar. How about Fred Smith Sr? No, not the guy who started FedEx. This Fred Smith ran a consulting firm, and Ziglar considered him a mentor. Smith says that passion for anything starts the moment you get a glimpse of the potential for the project, yourself, the mission, and so on. When you get that glimpse, the passion is born. Of course, this means you actually have to have an open mind and on the lookout so you actually can catch a glimpse. Ziglar breaks passion down into three steps: (1) Analyze what you want in life and develop a plan, (2) take steps toward those goals, and (3) use your head to work with your heart to gain maximum benefit.

My golf game is a good example here. Years ago I set a goal to be a single handicap. For years I couldn't do anything to really move toward that goal, but it was still there, while I worked on more pressing goals. When I got my chance, I started to play more. But want wasn't good enough. I needed to learn how to play better. I took lessons. As I write this, I am a nine handicap and have to continue to work at my game to keep it from decaying. Five years ago I was a twenty-five handicap. But life is about more than golf. Success at work comes with passion, too. Similarly, I enjoy speaking. I was pretty good at it and realized I could make a living doing it. But that didn't make me a professional speaker. I needed to work at it, but it didn't feel like work. I love what I do.

If you don't care about what is happening in your workplace, there is no way anyone else will care. When you do care, you get people fired up. The old cliché, "That which interests my boss fascinates me" sums this up nicely. If you aren't interested, they will not be fascinated. I would add, if you aren't passionate, they won't even care.

Nothing great in the world has ever been accomplished without passion. —Hegel

ZEAL IN ACTION

Most founders of construction firms are passionate about the business and what it exists to do. The industry is too challenging to be anything less. However, some founders stand out. Their passion and enthusiasm is infectious, and they are practically a force of nature. You cannot help but be swept up in their energy and drive for excellence. One such founder is Dan Baker.

Dan started pouring sidewalks with his brothers in 1968. Since then he has led the evolution and creation of one of the most respected specialty subcontractors in the United States. Baker Concrete Construction is among the largest and most successful in the country. It consistently ranks near the top of the ENR list of the top 600 specialty concrete contractors in the United States. Dan has a genuine respect for people and an unwavering love for the company and how it helps customers succeed. The diversity in the firm is testimony to his zeal. There are many coworkers whose resumes and styles don't fit the traditional "constructor" profile. Dan Baker recruited all of the members of the senior management team and is heavily involved in recruiting superintendents and college graduates. His ability to articulate a vision and to explain to people how they fit and how they can contribute gets them in the door. His confidence in them and his unbridled enthusiasm keeps them.

The firm has lower turnover and higher productivity than its peers, and its continued growth bodes well for future success. Dan Baker always tells his clients to "expect more," and his coworkers always find a way to deliver. Their success confirms that zeal goes a long way in motivating a team.

A TO Z APPLICATION

1. On a scale of 1–10, how do you rate on zeal? _____

2. About what are you most passionate? _____

_____

_____

_____

3. List someone you know who exemplifies this trait: _____

_____

4. What action *will* you do to improve in this area?_____

_____

_____

ZEAL JUMPSTART

- Develop goals and work to achieve them.
- Read *Real Success*.
- Spend time doing what energizes you; it creates more energy.
- Find ways to merge your passion and your work. (Do you even know what your passions are?)
- Smile.

ABOUT THE AUTHOR

Wally Adamchik is president of FireStarter Speaking and Consulting. His team speaks and consults on leadership with contractors across North America and he is a regular presenter at industry gatherings such as World of Concrete, ConExpo, and many others. He is noted for his ability to deliver dynamic, highly informative sessions.

FireStarter clients include some of the largest international firms on the ENR lists as well as small contractors working in local markets. Wally provides relevant and usable information to enable any size firm to be more competitive and more profitable. Solutions are based on his unique insights growing up in the industry, leading in the United States Marine Corps, managing his own business, and on his Master's work in business administration from the University of North Carolina at Chapel Hill. Before commissioning as a

Marine Corps officer, Wally graduated from the University of Notre Dame where he was the mascot during his senior year.

He holds the Certified Speaking Professional and the Certified Management Consultant designations and has held leadership positions in several associations. His passion for golf is exceeded only by his passion to create great leaders. Wally lives in Raleigh, North Caronlina.

ORDERING INFORMATION

Using the latest digital publishing technology, we are able to create and print custom copies of *Construction Leadership from A to Z* for your firm. There are three ways the book may be customized for your organization.

- Insert a personal introduction written by your president or CEO, addressed to your employees
- Add company-specific examples to increase impact on your readers
- Submit chapter edits to make content consistent with your corporate values

Additionally, we create customized follow-on training in the form of email blasts and/or videos that can be delivered straight to your desktop or portable device. The goal is to provide ongoing reinforcement that increases your ROI for leadership development by presenting content that employees know was created specifically for them.

Contact Wally Adamchick by email at Wally@beafirestarter. com and discuss how you can use *Construction Leadership from A to Z* meet your leadership development goals.